Heinemann **Shakespeare**

New Edition

Romeo and Juliet

SERIES EDITOR:
JOHN SEELY

EDITORIAL MATERIAL AND ACTIVITIES:
JOHN SEELY
RICHARD DURANT
ELIZABETH SEELY

Part of Pearson

Heinemann is an imprint of Pearson Education Limited, a company incorporated in England and Wales, having its registered office at Edinburgh Gate, Harlow, Essex, CM20 2JE. Registered company number: 872828

www.pearsonschoolsandfecolleges.co.uk

Heinemann is a registered trademark of Pearson Education Limited

First published 1993
This new edition published 2010

15
10 9 8 7

British Library Cataloguing in Publication Data
A catalogue record for this book is available from the British Library

ISBN 9780435026493

Original illustrations © Pearson Education Limited, 2005
Illustrated by Roger Wade Walker
Cover photo © Photostage Ltd
Printed and bound in China (CTPS /07)

Every effort has been made to contact copyright holders of material reproduced in this book. Any omissions will be rectified in subsequent printings if notice is given to the publishers.

CONTENTS

The story of the play

Act 1

Scene 1

There is a long-standing feud in Verona between two wealthy families, the Montagues and the Capulets. Their servants go about the streets with drawn swords, looking to start a fight with the other side. A quarrel develops, and Benvolio, a Montague, tries to part them. Now Tybalt, a Capulet, is drawn in and threatens Benvolio. They fight. More join in on either side. The noise brings Lord and Lady Capulet, and then Lord and Lady Montague to the scene. The Prince arrives, and reads the riot act. Lady Montague is relieved that her son Romeo was not involved, but both his parents are concerned about him. When Romeo appears he confesses to his friends that he is in love with Rosaline, but she is not interested. This explains his strange mood.

Scene 2

At the Capulet mansion, Paris, a wealthy young nobleman and a relation of the Prince, asks for permission to marry Juliet, Capulet's only daughter. He is invited to meet her at the feast that night.

Scene 3

Lady Capulet tells Juliet about Paris's proposal, and of the family's plans for her.

Scene 4

Benvolio persuades Romeo to gatecrash the feast, and Mercutio, another friend, joins in.

Scene 5

At the feast Romeo catches sight of Juliet and falls in love, but Tybalt has recognised him as one of the Montagues and prepares to fight. Lord Capulet holds him back, but Tybalt is furious and vows that this is not the end of it. Romeo and Juliet meet in the dance and kiss. She falls for him and is appalled when her Nurse tells her he is a Montague.

Act 2

Scene 1

After the feast Romeo's friends look for him and call his name, but Romeo has climbed into the Capulets' garden.

Scene 2

Romeo watches from the garden, as Juliet appears at her window. Although she is only speaking to herself she makes it clear that she has fallen in love with Romeo. He is madly in love with her – but he has the wrong family name. Before they part they vow to marry, and arrange to meet on the following day.

Scene 3

The next day Romeo goes to his priest, Friar Lawrence, to make his confession. Friar Lawrence is not happy at the sudden change in Romeo's affection from Rosaline to Juliet. However, because he hopes that a marriage between Juliet and Romeo may end the feuding between the two families, he agrees to marry them.

Scene 4

Juliet has sent her Nurse to find out what is planned, and Romeo tells her that Juliet must go to confession at Friar Lawrence's cell. There they will be married. Romeo's servant will give the Nurse a rope ladder so that the married pair can spend the night together.

Scene 5

The Nurse reports back to Juliet.

Scene 6

Friar Lawrence marries the two young lovers.

Act 3
Scene 1

In the street, Mercutio warns Benvolio against quarrelling with the Capulets. When Tybalt appears, it is Mercutio who stirs things up and Benvolio who tries to calm things down. Catching sight of Romeo, Tybalt insults him and Mercutio starts a fight. Romeo tries to stop them. As he moves between them, Mercutio is killed. Romeo then attacks Tybalt and kills him. When the Prince arrives, Benvolio explains what happened and the Prince sentences Romeo to be banished from Verona. If he is found there again he will be executed.

Scene 2

Juliet is horrified to learn that Romeo has been banished. Her Nurse promises to meet Romeo and arrange for him to visit to say goodbye.

Scene 3

Friar Lawrence and the Nurse try to comfort Romeo, and the Friar promises to try to help him.

Scene 4

At the Capulet mansion Juliet's father tells Paris that his wedding to Juliet will take place in three days' time.

Scene 5

Romeo and Juliet have spent the night together, but now Romeo must leave or he will be in danger. When he has gone Lady Capulet brings the news that Juliet is to marry Paris. Juliet refuses and when her father hears this he calls her terrible names and disowns her. Her mother agrees with her husband. Even the Nurse tries to persuade her to marry Paris although she knows that she is already married. Juliet leaves to go to Friar Lawrence's cell to ask for help.

Act 4
Scene 1

Paris goes to Friar Lawrence to explain that his marriage will be celebrated in the next few days. He has not been able to woo Juliet in the normal way because of Tybalt's death. Juliet arrives and refuses to treat Paris as her husband-to-be. When he leaves, she tells the Friar of her hopelessness and despair. The Friar then offers her a drug which will make it look as if she is dead. She will be laid to rest in the family burial chamber and when she wakes, Romeo will be by her side. The Friar will send this message to Mantua by Romeo's servant.

Scene 2

At the Capulet mansion arrangements for the wedding feast are going ahead. Juliet apologises for her disobedience to her father. He now brings the marriage forward to the following day.

Scene 3

When the wedding clothes have been chosen and the Nurse has left, Juliet hesitantly drinks the Friar's potion.

Scene 4

The following morning preparations for the wedding are in full swing and Paris arrives to greet his bride.

Scene 5

The Nurse finds she cannot wake Juliet up. They all believe she is dead and mourn her death. Friar Lawrence calms everyone down and arrangements are made for the funeral.

Act 5

Scene 1

Romeo's servant comes to him in Mantua with the news that Juliet is dead. Romeo orders a swift return to Verona. He has remembered seeing a poor chemist in ragged clothes who might sell him some poison. The man is reluctant because to sell poison carries the death penalty. Romeo's money persuades him to sell.

Scene 2

Friar Lawrence is horrified to discover that his letter to Romeo telling him that Juliet isn't really dead has not been delivered. His brother friar who had to carry the letter has been prevented from travelling by the authorities. They were afraid he might have been infected with the plague. Friar Lawrence sets off for Juliet's tomb.

Scene 3

Paris has already arrived at the tomb to mourn Juliet. He has left his servant to keep watch and he hears someone approach. Romeo and his servant have come with tools to break open the tomb. The servant is told to go away but he is concerned for Romeo and hides nearby. Paris interrupts Romeo as he opens the tomb, and provokes a fight. Paris is killed. As Paris falls, Romeo recognises him and lays him in the tomb. Juliet looks just as she did in life. Romeo sees Tybalt's body in the tomb and begs his forgiveness. He takes the poison he has bought, kisses Juliet and dies.

Friar Lawrence also intends to open the tomb but he is too late. Juliet awakes and sees Romeo dead. She refuses to listen to the Friar, who offers her life in a convent, takes Romeo's dagger and kills herself. The watchmen soon arrive to try to make sense of what has happened. Romeo's servant and the Friar are arrested. The Prince is roused and the Friar and Balthasar explain everything. This double tragedy at last brings the Montague and Capulet families together in grief, but with hope for the future.

Background to the play

Romeo and Juliet was first performed during the reign of Queen Elizabeth I between 1591 and 1596. Although the play is set in Italy, its background would have been very recognisable to its Elizabethan audiences.

Family life

This was a male-dominated (or patriarchal) society. The father was the head of the family and what he said went. He commanded everyone in the household; even his wife was expected to obey him. His power extended to marriage. In wealthy families like those of the Montagues and Capulets, marriages were arranged by the head of the family. It was often done to increase family wealth or to make an important alliance with another powerful family. This is not to say that children were treated like slaves or that their wishes were completely ignored; early in the play Capulet says that Juliet can have some say in whom she marries. It is only when she flatly refuses to go along with his wishes that he treats her like a possession.

Growing up

But when we come to Juliet's age, the play is not typical of Elizabethan society. Juliet is 13 but her father considers she is old enough to be married, and so does she. More than that: she considers it is all right to kiss Romeo the first time they meet. In fact most Elizabethan women of this class did not marry until they were in their twenties, and people at this time would have found Juliet's behaviour shocking (or, possibly, exciting, depending on their age and background).

Violence and feuds

The play is full of violence: sword fights, daggers and death by poison. It begins with a full-scale riot, and by the time it ends five of the major characters have died on stage. Elizabethan society was violent, too. Street fighting was common and when well-heeled young men had a difference of opinion they would often settle it by a duel. Wealthy families sometimes became locked in feuds, just like that of the Montagues and Capulets, in which they, their servants, and their allies would take up weapons and fight in public.

The Italian connection

The play is set in Italy. Feuding may have been common in England, but Italy was famous for it. At that time Italy was not one united country, but a series of small independent states, many of which were based on a city. Within these city states one or two families were often all-powerful and frequently ended up fighting each other. This aspect of Italian life was well known in England and some people found it fascinating, while most treated foreigners with a mixture of distrust and hostility.

Plague and death

In the sixteenth century people were terrified of the plague, a deadly disease which killed thousands and for which there was no known cure. It was spread by fleas carried by rats. The fleas transferred from the rats to human beings and bit them, thus transmitting the disease. The plague was also highly infectious so it could spread from one human being to another. Very few people survived the infection. So Mercutio's cry of 'A plague o' both your houses!' would have sent a shiver through the audience, who would also have instantly understood why the disease could have prevented Friar John from delivering Friar Lawrence's letter. Between 1591 and 1596, the period in which the play was first performed, there were four outbreaks of plague in London. So these references in the play would have been particularly powerful.

Religion

Elizabeth's England was a Protestant Christian country which had cut itself off from the Roman Catholic Church only a few years before. Roman Catholics were still considered a threat to security. The play is set in Italy, so the characters are Roman Catholic and a key figure is a priest, Friar Lawrence. Many of the audience would have been very suspicious of his behaviour and motives, especially when he marries Romeo and Juliet in secret and later schemes to make it appear that Juliet is dead. Elizabethans would also have been shocked by the fact that the two lovers commit suicide. They believed that people who committed suicide could never go to heaven but would spend eternity in hell.

Shakespeare's theatre

Nowadays entertainment is piped into people's houses – TV, the internet and radio provide hundreds of different programme choices every day. But in Shakespeare's time, people went out to be entertained. If you lived in a city like London you could go to the theatre.

But it wasn't the kind of theatre we know today. There was no electricity and the only artificial lighting was candles or torches, so plays had to be watched in daylight. This meant that the main part of the theatre was open to the skies.

Many of Shakespeare's plays were performed at the Globe Theatre. A modern replica of the Globe now stands on London's Bankside, close to where the original was built. By visiting the Globe Theatre you can discover what it was like to go to the theatre in Shakespeare's time.

Once you were inside, you would see that the ground plan was more or less circular: in *Henry V*, Shakespeare talks about 'the wooden O'. All around the outside were galleries where people could pay to sit on a wooden bench. From the galleries you looked down on the stage and – very important – you were under cover if it rained!

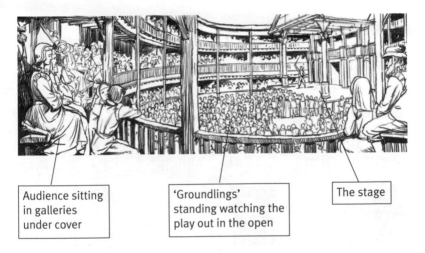

Audience sitting in galleries under cover

'Groundlings' standing watching the play out in the open

The stage

The stage measured about 12 metres by 12 metres. It was raised about 1.5 metres above the ground and was surrounded by a wide standing area. This was where the 'groundlings' went to watch the play. It was the cheapest way of seeing a play, but it meant that you had to stand for anything up to three hours. On the other hand, you were much closer to the action – the people at the front were close enough to touch the actors when they came to the edge of the stage.

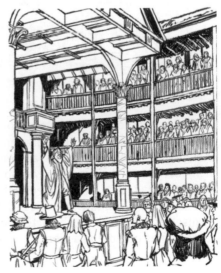

As you will see when you read the play, Shakespeare often gives the characters **soliloquies**, speeches which they make when alone on stage. Often they seem to be deliberately sharing their thoughts with the audience. When you look at the stage of the Globe and see how close the audience was, you realise how effective this must have been.

Some modern theatres have a curtain which hides the stage from the audience before the play and between scenes. This makes it easy to change the scenery without the audience seeing what is going on. In Shakespeare's theatre there was no curtain to conceal the main stage; the stage was always open to the audience. Very little scenery was used and if furniture was needed, the actors had to carry it on themselves. Similarly, if a character died on stage, the body had to be carried off as part of the action.

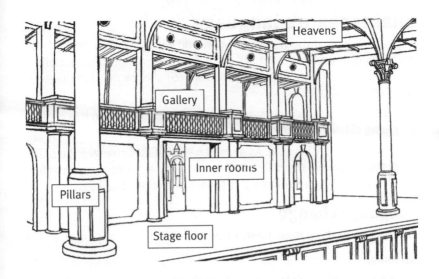

The stage was, however, quite complicated. Two large pillars on the main lower stage supported the roof, which was known as the 'heavens'. This kept the actors dry if it rained, but it could also be used for the action of the play. In some of the plays, Shakespeare has characters lowered from above down onto the stage. There were also trapdoors in the stage itself, so that people could suddenly appear from below. The heavens contained a space which could be used for sound effects. Cannons could be fired for battle scenes and cannon balls rolled along the floor to make the sound of thunder. At the back of the stage there was an inner room which could be concealed by a curtain. This was sometimes used for short scenes in the play. In *Romeo and Juliet*, this inner stage would have been used for Juliet's bedroom in Act 4 and the Capulet family tomb in Act 5. The gallery could be used by musicians, or as Juliet's balcony in Act 2.

Shakespeare's language

It is easy to look at the text of this play and say to yourself, 'I'm never going to understand that!' but it is important not to be put off. Remember that there are two reasons why Shakespeare's language may seem strange at first:

1   He was writing 400 years ago and the English language has changed over the centuries.

2   He wrote mainly in **verse**. As a result he sometimes changed the order of words to make them fit the **verse** form, and he used a large number of 'tricks of the trade': figures of speech and other techniques.

Language change

This can cause three main kinds of problem:

Grammar

Since the end of the sixteenth century, there have been some changes in English grammar. Some examples:

1   ***Thee, thou, thy***, *and the verb forms that go with them:*
>   *O gentle Romeo,*
> *If **thou dost** love, pronounce it faithfully.*
> *Or if **thou thinkest** I am too quickly won,*
> *I'll frown, and be perverse, and say **thee** nay,*
> *So **thou wilt** woo*

2   Words contract (shorten) in different ways. Some examples of **contractions**:
    'tis rather than *it's*
    who is't for *who is it*

3   Some of the 'little words' are different. For example: *an* for *if*.

Words that have changed their meaning

Sometimes you will come across words that you think you know, but then discover that they don't mean what you expect them to mean. For example: *presently* (Act 4 scene 1 line 54) meant *at once* in Shakespeare's day. Now it means *in a while*. Nowadays if you are fond of someone, you like them quite a lot. But in Act 2 scene 2 line 98, it means *excessively, madly in love*.

Words that have gone out of use

These are the most obvious and most frequent causes of difficulty. Shakespeare had – and used – a huge vocabulary. He loved using words, and pushing them to their limits. So you will come across many words you have not met before. These are explained in the notes on the page facing the play text.

The language of the play

Most of *Romeo and Juliet* is in **blank verse**, but parts are in **prose** and short sections are in **rhymed verse**.

Blank verse

The main part of the play is written in lines of ten syllables, with a repeated even pattern of weak and strong 'beats':
*In **fair** Verona **where** we **lay** our **scene***
(ti **tum** ti **tum** ti **tum** ti **tum** ti **tum**)

The line divides into five sections, each with a weak and a strong beat. This is called an **iambic pentameter**.

If Shakespeare had made every line exactly the same, the play would soon become very monotonous, so he varies the rhythm in a number of ways. Often he just changes the pattern of weak and strong slightly:

Which**, but their **child**ren's **end naught** could re**move
(**tum** ti ti **tum** ti **tum tum** ti ti **tum**)

He also writes so that sentences sometimes end at the end of a line, and at other times in the middle:

God's bread! It makes me mad.
Day, night; hour, tide, time; work, play;
Alone, in company; still my care hath been
To have her matched.

So the verse of the play has a strong but varied **rhythm**. Most of the lines do not rhyme, so they are 'blank', hence the term blank verse.

Rhymed verse

Sometimes Shakespeare uses a pattern of rhymed lines. It may be just two successive lines (a rhyming couplet):

ROMEO   Farewell, thou canst not teach me to for**get**.

BENVOLIO   I'll pay that doctrine, or else die in **debt**.

Rhyming couplets often round off a scene, but they are also used in the middle of scenes. Sometimes there is a more complicated pattern of rhymes:

ROMEO   When the devout religion of mine **eye**   A
         Maintains such falsehood, then turn tears to <u>fires</u>,   B
         And these who often drowned could never **die**,   A
         Transparent heretics, be burnt for <u>liars</u>.   B
         One fairer than my love? The all-seeing *sun*   C
         Ne'er saw her match since first the world *begun*.   C

Here the first and third lines rhyme, and so do the second and fourth. Then the fifth and sixth lines rhyme. We can describe this pattern of rhyming by saying that the 'rhyme scheme' is: ABAB CC. This pattern is taken from the sonnet, a popular form for love poems.

A sonnet was a 14-line poem with the following rhyme scheme:

ABAB CDCD EFEF GG.

Prose

In some scenes, characters' speeches are not written in blank or rhymed verse, but in 'ordinary sentences': prose. Some characters in the play speak only in prose – for example the Nurse. Some characters speak verse at times and prose at others: it depends on the situation. So when Romeo talks about love he speaks verse, but when he is having a battle of wits with Mercutio, he speaks prose.

Romeo and Juliet

Characters

ESCALUS, Prince of Verona

PARIS, a nobleman, kinsman to the Prince

MONTAGUE
CAPULET } heads of two opposed Houses

SECOND CAPULET, cousin to Capulet

ROMEO, son to Montague

BENVOLIO, nephew to Montague and friend to Romeo

MERCUTIO, kinsman to the Prince and friend to Romeo

TYBALT, nephew to Lady Capulet

PETRUCHIO, a Capulet and friend to Tybalt

FRIAR LAWRENCE
FRIAR JOHN } Franciscans

BALTHASAR, servant to Romeo

ABRAHAM, servant to Montague

SAMPSON
GREGORY } servants to Capulet

PETER, a clown, servant to the Nurse

ANTHONY
POTPAN } servants to Capulet

AN APOTHECARY

PAGE to Paris

CHORUS

LADY MONTAGUE, wife to Montague

LADY CAPULET, wife to Capulet

JULIET, daughter to Capulet

NURSE to Juliet

Attendants, Citizens, Musicians, Servants, Watchmen.

Scene: *Verona*; *Mantua*; *Friar Lawrence's cell*

The prologue, spoken by one of the actors, introduces the play and sums up what is going to happen. We know from the very beginning that the play will end in tragedy: two noble families in Verona have been fighting each other for a long time. Two teenagers, one from each family, fall in love. But it is only by their deaths that the conflict between their families comes to an end.

1–14 This speech takes the form of a **sonnet** (see p. 14): a poem with a complicated rhyming pattern.

1 **both alike in dignity** of similar (high) social status

2 **where ... scene** where the play takes place

3 **ancient grudge** an old disagreement

new mutiny a new conflict

4 **civil** They are civilians, not soldiers, but it also a **pun** (see Glossary p. 292): if you are 'civil' to someone you are polite to them, and this is the exact opposite.

blood This is the first of many references to blood and death.

5–6 **From ... life** These two hostile but ill-fated families have two children who fall in love; they, too, are destined to end their lives unhappily

7 **misadventured ... overthrows** unfortunate and pitiful deaths

8 **Doth ... strife** end the conflict between their parents by their own deaths

9 **passage** course

11 **but** except for

nought nothing

12 **two hours' ... stage** the subject matter of the play, lasting two hours (In fact the play is considerably longer than two hours, but the expression is probably just meant to show that the play is not going to be boring.)

13–14 **The which ... mend** and if you listen patiently we will work hard to fill in the gaps in the story I have just told you

Prologue

CHORUS

Two households both alike in dignity,
In fair Verona where we lay our scene,
From ancient grudge break to new mutiny.
Where civil blood makes civil hands unclean.
From forth the fatal loins of these two foes   5
A pair of star-crossed lovers take their life;
Whose misadventured piteous overthrows
Doth with their death bury their parents' strife.
The fearful passage of their death-marked love,
And the continuance of their parents' rage,   10
Which, but their children's end, nought could remove,
Is now the two hours' traffic of our stage;
The which if you with patient ears attend,
What here shall miss, our toil shall strive to mend.

[Exit

It is a hot summer's day in Verona. Two servants of the Capulet family are swaggering around the streets. They are wearing swords and looking for a fight. They boast about what they will do if they meet servants of the Montague family.

Much of this scene is in **prose** (see p. 14) and the two servants make use of many rude and offensive **puns**.

SD **swords and bucklers** They are carrying weapons suitable for servants: heavy swords and small round shields

1 **carry coals** put up with insults

2 **colliers** men selling coal in the streets

3 **an we be** if we are

choler A pun on the word 'collier' but it means 'anger'.

4 **collar** Another pun: Sampson should not leave his neck in the hangman's noose, and avoid doing anything which might be punished by execution.

5 **I strike ... moved** If I get angry I hit out

8 **stir** run away

valiant brave

stand hold your ground (but also a pun about his manhood)

12 **take the wall** take a superior position, away from the dirt in the central gutter

13–14 **the weakest ... wall** the loser in a struggle: a **proverb** (see Glossary p. 291)

15–16 **women ... vessels** A 'vessel' used to mean 'a body as container' and a woman's body would be considered weaker than a man's.

21–3 **When ... maids** After fighting the men, Sampson will 'deal with' the women.

26 **maidenheads** virginity

Act One

Scene ❶

Verona. A public place
Enter SAMPSON *and* GREGORY, *of the house of*
Capulet, with swords and bucklers

SAMPSON	Gregory, on my word, we'll not carry coals.
GREGORY	No, for then we should be colliers.
SAMPSON	I mean, an we be in choler, we'll draw.
GREGORY	Ay, while you live, draw your neck out of collar.
SAMPSON	I strike quickly being moved.
GREGORY	But thou art not quickly moved to strike.
SAMPSON	A dog of the house of Montague moves me.
GREGORY	To move is to stir, and to be valiant is to stand. Therefore, if thou art moved thou runn'st away.
SAMPSON	A dog of that house shall move me to stand. I will take the wall of any man or maid of Montague's.
GREGORY	That shows thee a weak slave, for the weakest goes to the wall.
SAMPSON	'Tis true, and therefore women being the weaker vessels are ever thrust to the wall. Therefore I will push Montague's men from the wall, and thrust his maids to the wall.
GREGORY	The quarrel is between our masters, and us their men.
SAMPSON	'Tis all one. I will show myself a tyrant. When I have fought with the men, I will be civil with the maids – I will cut off their heads.
GREGORY	The heads of the maids?
SAMPSON	Ay, the heads of the maids, or their maidenheads – take it in what sense thou wilt.

5

10

15

20

25

Gregory and Sampson meet two servants from the house of Montague and begin to make fun of them, looking for trouble.

27–32 **They ... Montagues** Sampson and Gregory continue to boast, using words with double meaning suggesting sexual activity.

31 **poor-john** salted and dried hake, a cheap fish

tool sword (with the obvious double meaning)

33 **Quarrel** Make a quarrel, start an argument

35 **Fear me not** I won't let you down

36 **marry** Originally this was short for 'By the Virgin Mary', but it was only a mild thing to say (like 'indeed').

37 **Let ... sides** Let us stay on the right side of the law

38 **frown** sneer, make a face

39 **list** wish

40 **bite my thumb** A rude gesture: you put your thumb in your mouth and then withdrew it, clicking the nail against your upper front teeth.

45 **Is ... side** It is very important not to be the one who starts the fight, otherwise they will be in trouble with the law.

SD **BENVOLIO** The name means 'well-wishing' in Italian.

GREGORY	They must take it in sense that feel it.
SAMPSON	Me they shall feel while I am able to stand, and 'tis known I am a pretty piece of flesh.
GREGORY	'Tis well thou art not fish; if thou hadst, thou 30 hadst been poor-john. Draw thy tool, here comes of the house of Montagues.

Enter two other serving-men, ABRAHAM *and* BALTHASAR

SAMPSON	My naked weapon is out. Quarrel, I will back thee.
GREGORY	How, turn thy back and run?
SAMPSON	Fear me not. 35
GREGORY	No marry, I fear thee!
SAMPSON	Let us take the law of our sides, let them begin.
GREGORY	I will frown as I pass by, and let them take it as they list.
SAMPSON	Nay, as they dare. I will bite my thumb at them, 40 which is disgrace to them if they bear it.
ABRAHAM	Do you bite your thumb at us sir?
SAMPSON	I do bite my thumb sir.
ABRAHAM	Do you bite your thumb at us sir?
SAMPSON	[*Aside to* GREGORY] Is the law of our side if I say 45 'Ay'.
GREGORY	[*Aside to* SAMPSON] No.
SAMPSON	No sir, I do not bite my thumb at you sir, but I bite my thumb sir.
GREGORY	Do you quarrel sir? 50
ABRAHAM	Quarrel sir? No sir.
SAMPSON	But if you do sir, I am for you. I serve as good a man as you.
ABRAHAM	No better.
SAMPSON	Well sir. 55

Enter BENVOLIO

The argument between the servants develops into a fight. Benvolio, a Montague, tries to stop the fighting, but Tybalt, one of the Capulets, arrives and attacks him. Citizens come and try to stop the fighting but then the leader of the Capulet family arrives and wants to join in too. He is held back by his wife.

57   **kinsmen** relatives

61   **washing blow** slashing cut

63   Here the language moves from **prose** to **verse** (see p. 14).

       Put up Sheathe

64   **heartless hinds** A **play on words**: 'heartless' means without a male deer (hart) to protect them; 'hinds' are literally female deer, but also female servants.

66   **I do but keep** I'm only keeping

67   **manage it to part** use it to separate

SD   *They fight* There is a description of what happens in lines 107–13.

71   **Clubs ... partisans!** Weapons: bills and partisans are kinds of pike (a long spear that was held and thrust, rather than thrown).

75   **A crutch** She means that rather than having a sword, he is so old he ought to be asking for a crutch to support him.

77   **in spite of** in hatred of

78–9   **Thou ... foe** These two lines are rhymed. They lead in to the arrival of the Prince, and a more formal, stately section after all the excitement and coarseness that has gone before.

79   **stir** move

GREGORY	[*Aside to* SAMPSON] Say 'better'; here comes one of my master's kinsmen.
SAMPSON	Yes, better sir.
ABRAHAM	You lie.
SAMPSON	Draw if you be men. Gregory, remember thy 60 washing blow.

[They fight

BENVOLIO	Part fools. Put up your swords! You know not what you do.

Enter TYBALT.

TYBALT	What, art thou drawn among these heartless hinds? 65 Turn thee Benvolio, look upon thy death.
BENVOLIO	I do but keep the peace. Put up thy sword, Or manage it to part these men with me.
TYBALT	What, drawn and talk of peace? I hate the word, As I hate hell, all Montagues, and thee. Have at thee, coward! 70

[They fight

Enter OFFICER *and Citizens with clubs and partisans*

OFFICER	Clubs, bills and partisans! Strike, beat them down. Down with the Capulets! Down with the Montagues!

Enter OLD CAPULET, *in his gown, and* LADY CAPULET

CAPULET	What noise is this? Give me my long sword, ho!
L. CAPULET	A crutch, a crutch! Why call you for a sword? 75
CAPULET	My sword I say! Old Montague is come, And flourishes his blade in spite of me.

Enter OLD MONTAGUE *and* LADY MONTAGUE

MONTAGUE	Thou villain Capulet! Hold me not, let me go.
L. MONTAGUE	Thou shalt not stir one foot to seek a foe.

Enter PRINCE ESCALUS, *with his train*

23

Just as the head of the house of Montague is also attempting to join the fray, the Prince of Verona arrives and quells the riot. He orders them all to put down their weapons and tells Capulet and Montague that if anyone ever disturbs the peace again in this way they will be executed. Benvolio tells Montague how the fight began.

81	**Profaners ... steel** They have stained the steel of their swords with the blood of their fellow-citizens (neighbours) and, in this way they have abused or polluted (profaned) it.
83	**pernicious** destructive
85	**On pain of torture** Unless they do as they are ordered they will be punished.
86	**mistempered** A **play on words**: 'temper' means 1) the toughness of a piece of metal after it has been tempered 2) angry mood. So if the weapons are 'mistempered' they have been 1) made for the wrong purpose 2) used in anger.
87	**moved** angry
88	**civil brawls** fights between citizens
	bred ... word started because of a stupid remark
92	**Cast ... ornaments** put down the sober (and suitable) things they were carrying
93	**to wield old ... old** to brandish old spears in hands that are as old as the spears
94	**Cankered** The spears have grown rusty because they have not been used for so long. The citizens have been at peace for many years and are not used to fighting.
	cankered hate hatred that is misshapen like a cankered plant
96	**Your ... forfeit** you will be executed
100	**our further pleasure** what else I have decided
103	**Who ... abroach?** Who started up this old quarrel again?
104	**by** nearby
106	**close fighting** fighting hand to hand
107	**drew** drew my sword
111	**nothing hurt withal** not at all hurt by it

PRINCE Rebellious subjects, enemies to peace,   80
        Profaners of this neighbour-stained steel –
        Will they not hear? – What ho! You men, you beasts,
        That quench the fire of your pernicious rage
        With purple fountains issuing from your veins,
        On pain of torture, from those bloody hands   85
        Throw your mistempered weapons to the ground,
        And hear the sentence of your moved Prince.
        Three civil brawls bred of an airy word
        By thee old Capulet, and Montague,
        Have thrice disturbed the quiet of our streets,   90
        And made Verona's ancient citizens
        Cast by their grave beseeming ornaments,
        To wield old partisans, in hands as old,
        Cankered with peace, to part your cankered hate.
        If ever you disturb our streets again,   95
        Your lives shall pay the forfeit of the peace.
        For this time all the rest depart away.
        You Capulet shall go along with me.
        And Montague, come you this afternoon,
        To know our further pleasure in this case,   100
        To old Freetown, our common judgement-place.
        Once more, on pain of death, all men depart.
        [Exeunt all but MONTAGUE, LADY MONTAGUE, *and*
                                                BENVOLIO

MONTAGUE Who set this ancient quarrel new abroach?
          Speak nephew, were you by when it began?

BENVOLIO Here were the servants of your adversary,   105
          And yours, close fighting ere I did approach.
          I drew to part them; in the instant came
          The fiery Tybalt, with his sword prepared,
          Which as he breathed defiance to my ears,
          He swung about his head and cut the winds,   110
          Who nothing hurt withal hissed him in scorn.
          While we were interchanging thrusts and blows,
          Came more and more and fought on part and part,
          Till the Prince came, who parted either part.

Lady Montague asks where her son, Romeo, is. Benvolio has seen him and describes how he has seen him wandering around like a typical love-sick young man. Romeo just wants to be left alone. No one seems to know what is the matter with him.

117–18 **an hour ... east** an hour before dawn

117 **worshipped sun** The sun is referred to as if it were a god: **personification** (see Glossary p. 291).

119 **abroad** out and about

123 **made** walked

was ware of noticed

124 **covert** hiding-place

125–6 **I, measuring ... found** I recognised that his mood was like mine: we both wanted to be alone

128 **Pursued ... his** went along with my own mood by not following him

129 **shunned** avoided a person

131 **augmenting** adding to

135 **Aurora's bed** Aurora is the goddess of dawn (**personification** again).

136 **heavy** sad

137 **pens himself** shuts himself up

140 **portentous** ominous, worrying

141 **counsel** advice

144 **importuned him** pressed him to explain

146 **his ... counsellor** he will only listen to his own advice about his feelings

147 **true** honest

148 **so secret ... close** uncommunicative and private

149 **So far ... discovery** a long way from sorting out the depth of his feelings and speaking about it

L. MONTAGUE	O where is Romeo? Saw you him today?	115
	Right glad I am he was not at this fray.	
BENVOLIO	Madam, an hour before the worshipped sun	
	Peered forth the golden window of the east,	
	A troubled mind drive me to walk abroad,	
	Where underneath the grove of sycamore,	120
	That westward rooteth from this city side,	
	So early walking did I see your son.	
	Towards him I made; but he was ware of me,	
	And stole into the covert of the wood.	
	I, measuring his affections by my own,	125
	Which then most sought where most might not	
	be found,	
	Being one too many by my weary self,	
	Pursued my humour, not pursuing his,	
	And gladly shunned who gladly fled from me.	
MONTAGUE	Many a morning hath he there been seen,	130
	With tears augmenting the fresh morning's dew,	
	Adding to clouds more clouds with his deep sighs,	
	But all so soon as the all-cheering sun	
	Should in the farthest east begin to draw	
	The shady curtains from Aurora's bed,	135
	Away from light steals home my heavy son,	
	And private in his chamber pens himself,	
	Shuts up his windows, locks fair daylight out,	
	And makes himself an artificial night.	
	Black and portentous must this humour prove,	140
	Unless good counsel may the cause remove.	
BENVOLIO	My noble uncle, do you know the cause?	
MONTAGUE	I neither know it, nor can learn of him.	
BENVOLIO	Have you importuned him by any means?	
MONTAGUE	Both by myself and many other friends.	145
	But he, his own affections' counsellor,	
	Is to himself – I will not say how true –	
	But to himself so secret and so close,	
	So far from sounding and discovery,	

Romeo arrives and his parents withdraw. Benvolio asks him why he is so sad. Romeo explains that he is in love and feels completely confused.

150–1   **As is ... air** a flower bud may already have a grub inside it, spoiling or destroying it before it can open

154   **We ... know** our desire to know why he is so sad is every bit as strong as our desire to help him through his problems

156   **be much denied** put up with his determined refusal to tell me

158   **shrift** confession

160   **But new** Only just

163   **Not ... short** The fact that I haven't got what would make time pass quickly if I did have it

168–9   **so gentle ... proof!** so gentle to look at turns out to be oppressive and cruel when we experience it!

170   **whose view is muffled** Cupid, the god of love, was often painted as blindfolded.

171   **to his will** to getting his own way

172   **Where shall we dine?** Romeo is, perhaps, trying to change the subject.

175–9   **o brawling ... health** At the time when Shakespeare wrote *Romeo and Juliet*, it was fashionable for poets to write of love using apparently impossible opposites like 'loving hate'. These opposites are called **oxymorons** (see Glossary p. 291). This part of the speech shows how confused Romeo's feelings are (or is it that he wants to seem confused?)

175–6   These two lines are rhymed, and so are lines 155–60 and 170–1. This use of rhyme makes the speeches sound more formal and 'poetic', which is very suitable in a section describing the sadness of being in love.

176   **O any ... create!** like the first thing to be made, created by God out of nothing!

As is the bud bit with an envious worm,   150
Ere he can spread his sweet leaves to the air,
Or dedicate his beauty to the sun.
Could we but learn from whence his sorrows grow,
We would as willingly give cure as know.

Enter ROMEO

BENVOLIO	See where he comes. So please you step aside. 155
	I'll know his grievance or be much denied.
MONTAGUE	I would thou wert so happy by thy stay,
	To hear true shrift. Come, madam, let's away.

[*Exeunt* MONTAGUE, *and* LADY MONTAGUE

BENVOLIO	Good morrow cousin.
ROMEO	Is the day so young?
BENVOLIO	But new struck nine.
ROMEO	Ay me, sad hours seem long. 160
	Was that my father that went hence so fast?
BENVOLIO	It was. What sadness lengthens Romeo's hours?
ROMEO	Not having that which having makes them short.
BENVOLIO	In love?
ROMEO	Out – 165
BENVOLIO	Of love?
ROMEO	Out of her favour where I am in love.
BENVOLIO	Alas that love, so gentle in his view,
	Should be so tyrannous and rough in proof!
ROMEO	Alas that love, whose view is muffled still, 170
	Should without eyes see pathways to his will.
	Where shall we dine? O me, what fray was here?
	Yet tell me not, for I have heard it all.
	Here's much to do with hate, but more with love.
	Why then, o brawling love, o loving hate, 175
	O any thing of nothing first create!
	O heavy lightness, serious vanity,
	Mis-shapen chaos of well-seeming forms,
	Feather of lead, bright smoke, cold fire, sick health,

Benvolio tries without success to discover the name of the girl Romeo has fallen in love with. Romeo explains that she is not in love with him.

183   **oppression** distress, depression

184–93 This speech is written in pairs of rhymed lines, which seems suitable for a speech describing Romeo's feelings about love (or perhaps he just feels that it is suitable!) There is similar use of rhyme in lines 201–2 and 206–10.

184   **such ... transgression** love's sin is so great

186–7   **Which ... thine** you will increase my distress if you add your unhappiness to it

189   **fume** vapour

190   **Being purged** when we are rid of love

191   **Being vexed** when love is disturbed

192   **else** otherwise

    A madness most discreet Romeo is in love and is expressing the contradictions he feels.

    discreet cautious, careful

193   **choking gall** bitterness, poisonous substance

    preserving sweet sweetness making life seem more bearable

194   **coz** family member, kinsman

201   **Bid ... will?** How could you suggest to a man who is sick that he should make his will?

205   **mark-man** someone who knows how to aim well

206   **right fair mark** a beautiful target

207–8   **She'll ... arrow** The woman he has fallen in love with has decided that she will never fall in love.

208   **Cupid** the god of love

    Dian's wit the wisdom of Diana, the goddess of chastity

	Still-waking sleep, that is not what it is!	180
	This love feel I, that feel no love in this.	
	Dost thou not laugh?	
BENVOLIO	No coz, I rather weep.	
ROMEO	Good heart, at what?	
BENVOLIO	At thy good heart's oppression.	
ROMEO	Why such is love's transgression.	
	Griefs of mine own lie heavy in my breast,	185
	Which thou wilt propagate to have it pressed	
	With more of thine. This love that thou hast shown	
	Doth add more grief to too much of mine own.	
	Love is a smoke made with the fume of sighs,	
	Being purged, a fire sparkling in lovers' eyes,	190
	Being vexed, a sea nourished with lovers' tears,	
	What is it else? A madness most discreet,	
	A choking gall, and a preserving sweet.	
	Farewell my coz.	
BENVOLIO	Soft, I will go along.	
	And if you leave me so, you do me wrong.	195
ROMEO	Tut I have lost myself; I am not here.	
	This is not Romeo, he's some other where.	
BENVOLIO	Tell me in sadness, who is that you love.	
ROMEO	What, shall I groan and tell thee?	
BENVOLIO	Groan? Why no.	
	But sadly tell me who.	200
ROMEO	Bid a sick man in sadness make his will?	
	A word ill urged to one that is so ill.	
	In sadness cousin, I do love a woman.	
BENVOLIO	I aimed so near, when I supposed you loved.	
ROMEO	A right good mark-man. And she's fair I love.	205
BENVOLIO	A right fair mark, fair coz, is soonest hit.	
ROMEO	Well in that hit you miss. She'll not be hit	
	With Cupid's arrow. She hath Dian's wit,	
	And in strong proof of chastity well-armed,	

Benvolio tells Romeo he should forget about her and look at other girls.
Romeo says that is impossible. They leave.

210 **love's ... bow** Cupid is often painted as a chubby baby boy with a bow and arrows.

uncharmed not affected by the spell cast by Cupid's arrows

211 **stay ... terms** listen to any declarations of love

212 **bide ... eyes** allow me to enjoy looking at her

213 **ope ... gold** accept presents from me

215 **That ... store** because she will not marry and have children her beauty will never be reproduced

216 **still** forever

217–19 She ... posterity This is the same idea as in line 215.

220–1 She ... despair It is not right that her great beauty combined with her intention not to marry should lead me to despair (the unforgivable sin) and so to hell, whereas she will still deserve heaven

222 **forsworn to love** made a vow not to love

226–7 By ... beauties Let your eyes be free to look at other beautiful women

227–8 'Tis ... more Romeo says that if he does this, he will only see women who are less beautiful and this will just call to mind her amazing beauty.

229–30 These ... fair In the same way black carnival masks worn by women remind us that in fact they are hiding their true beauty

231–2 He ... lost A man who suddenly becomes blind cannot forget how precious his eyesight was

233 **passing fair** extremely beautiful

234–5 What ... fair? what is the point of her beauty except to remind me of someone who is even more beautiful?

237 **I'll ... debt** Benvolio takes up the challenge that he will not be able to persuade Romeo to forget his love.

	From love's weak childish bow she lives	
	uncharmed.	210
	She will not stay the siege of loving terms,	
	Nor bide th' encounter of assailing eyes,	
	Nor ope her lap to saint-seducing gold.	
	O she is rich in beauty, only poor,	
	That when she dies, with beauty dies her store.	215

BENVOLIO   Then she hath sworn that she will still live chaste?

ROMEO   She hath, and in that sparing makes huge waste;
For beauty starved with her severity,
Cuts beauty off from all posterity.
She is too fair, too wise; wisely too fair,   220
To merit bliss by making me despair.
She hath forsworn to love, and in that vow
Do I live dead that live to tell it now.

BENVOLIO   Be ruled by me, forget to think of her.

ROMEO   O teach me how I should forget to think.   225

BENVOLIO   By giving liberty unto thine eyes.
Examine other beauties.

ROMEO   'Tis the way
To call hers, exquisite, in question more.
These happy masks that kiss fair ladies' brows,
Being black, puts us in mind they hide the fair.   230
He that is strucken blind cannot forget
The precious treasure of his eyesight lost.
Show me a mistress that is passing fair,
What doth her beauty serve, but as a note
Where I may read who passed that passing fair?   235
Farewell, thou canst not teach me to forget.

BENVOLIO   I'll pay that doctrine, or else die in debt.

                         [*Exeunt*

Act 1 scene 1

The back story

The play begins with the Chorus telling us the back story. Copy the table below and fill in the missing details.

Chorus tells us:	The details
Who the story is about	
Where it happens	
What happens	
Why it happens	
How it ends	

Who's who

At the beginning of *Romeo and Juliet* we meet a lot of different people and we have to work out who they all are and think about how they might fit into the story. One way of getting a grip on who is who is to divide the characters into groups according to which side they are on.

1 Make a list of the 12 named characters who appear in Act 1 scene 1.

2 Copy the diagram below. Write the name of each character in the right group.

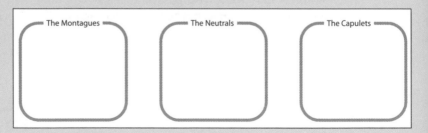

The Montagues   The Neutrals   The Capulets

The big fight

The play starts with a bang: a fight that almost turns into a riot. Lines
50–82 describe what happens. To help you visualise the sequence of
events, read these lines again, and then copy and complete this table,
filling in the blanks.

Tip: Look also at lines 105–14 for Benvolio's version of events.

Lines	Main characters	What they did
50–5	Gregory, Sampson, Abraham, Balthasar	*They square up to each other and trade insults*
	Benvolio	
56–61	Gregory, Sampson, Abraham, Balthasar	
62–3		
	Tybalt	
64–70	Benvolio, Tybalt	
	more Montagues more Capulets	
71–3	Officer, citizens	
74–7		
78–9		
80–2	Prince	

What's the matter with Romeo?

We hear about Romeo before we see him. In lines 115–54 Benvolio talks to Romeo's parents about their son.

Work with a partner

1 **a** Read the lines together.

   b Look at these possible statements about Romeo.

   He might kill himself.   He is a loner.
   No one loves him.   He is unhappy.
   He is sick of love.   He is selfish.

   c Decide which **two** of the statements are most true of Romeo.

   d Find evidence to support each of your two choices.

2 **Line 159 to the end of the scene:** Read these lines together and then look back at the six statements above. Decide which two you now think are most true of Romeo. Find evidence to support each of your two choices.

3 Romeo talks a lot about love in these lines. Here are four statements about Romeo's attitude. Discuss them and agree a rank order from most to least true.

   Love is painful.   Love is full of contradictions.
   Love is cruel.   We'd be better off without love.

Role play

Work with a partner: one of you is Benvolio; the other is Montague

Benvolio: Give your report to Montague on what you have found out about what is wrong with his son Romeo.

Montague: How do you respond?

Group discussion

What do we learn about Romeo from this scene? Think about:

- what Romeo says
- what others say about him.

Quotation quiz

For each of these quotations, work out:

1 who said it
2 who they were speaking to
3 what it tells us about
   a the speaker
   b any other characters.

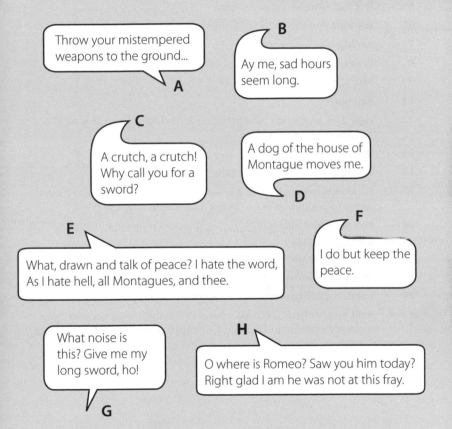

A
Throw your mistempered weapons to the ground...

B
Ay me, sad hours seem long.

C
A crutch, a crutch! Why call you for a sword?

D
A dog of the house of Montague moves me.

E
What, drawn and talk of peace? I hate the word, As I hate hell, all Montagues, and thee.

F
I do but keep the peace.

G
What noise is this? Give me my long sword, ho!

H
O where is Romeo? Saw you him today? Right glad I am he was not at this fray.

Capulet talks to Paris, a wealthy young man of Verona, about his daughter Juliet. Paris is asking for Juliet's hand in marriage and although Capulet is not unwilling, he thinks Juliet is too young; Paris should wait another two years. Paris is unhappy at this, so Capulet agrees that he can woo his daughter; if she is willing, then they will talk again. He invites Paris to the feast he is giving that evening; he will meet Juliet then.

1   **bound** (to keep the peace)

2   **In penalty alike** under threat of the same punishment (death)

4   **Of honourable reckoning** Of good reputation

5   **lived at odds** lived as enemies

6   **my suit** Paris has asked Capulet if he can marry Juliet.

7   **saying o'er** repeating

8   **is yet ... world** has lived a sheltered life

9   **She ... years** she is not yet 14

11   **Ere** before

        ripe This is the first of several images which compare young women to growing plants.

13   **marred** spoiled

14   **Earth ... she** All Capulet's other children have died.

16–37   Capulet speaks in rhyming couplets (see p. 14) which gives this section a formal feeling – as if it's all carefully worked out.

18   **she agreed** if she agrees

18–19   **within ... voice** I will give my consent and happy agreement to her marrying the man she chooses

22   **among the store** will be one of them

25   **Earth-treading stars** Capulet's distinguished guests

27–8   **well-apparelled ... treads** after a dull winter, well-dressed April suddenly appears in bud and leaf (April is personified as a young woman.)

Scene ❷

Enter CAPULET, PARIS, *and* PETER

CAPULET	But Montague is bound as well as I,
	In penalty alike; and 'tis not hard, I think,
	For men so old as we to keep the peace.
PARIS	Of honourable reckoning are you both,
	And pity 'tis you lived at odds so long. 5
	But now my lord, what say you to my suit?
CAPULET	But saying o'er what I have said before.
	My child is yet a stranger in the world,
	She hath not seen the change of fourteen years.
	Let two more summers wither in their pride 10
	Ere we may think her ripe to be a bride.
PARIS	Younger than she are happy mothers made.
CAPULET	And too soon marred are those so early made.
	Earth hath swallowed all my hopes but she,
	She is the hopeful lady of my earth. 15
	But woo her gentle Paris, get her heart,
	My will to her consent is but a part.
	And she agreed, within her scope of choice
	Lies my consent and fair according voice.
	This night I hold an old accustomed feast, 20
	Whereto I have invited many a guest,
	Such as I love; and you among the store,
	One more, most welcome, makes my number more.
	At my poor house look to behold this night
	Earth-treading stars that make dark heaven light. 25
	Such comfort as do lusty young men feel,
	When well-apparelled April on the heel

The servant is sent off with a list of guests to invite, but he can't read. Benvolio and Romeo return.

28   **even such delight** just such pleasure

29   **fresh female buds** pretty young women (again compared to growing plants)

29–30   **shall ... Inherit** you will enjoy this evening

30–3   **Hear ... none** Capulet encourages Paris to look and listen, and admire most the young woman who most deserves it. Once Paris has observed all the young women, there will be many he will like – including Capulet's daughter Juliet, and none better than her. Capulet is looking for a suitable husband for his daughter.

34   **sirrah** a usual form of address to servants

35   **find those persons out** look for these people

37   **on their pleasure stay** are waiting for the pleasure of their company

38–42   **Find ... nets** The servant, Peter, cannot carry out this task. As he confesses to us that he can't read, he muddles the tools of various trades.

40   **yard** measuring rod

       last the block on which shoes are formed

46–7   **one fire ... anguish** one fire will put another one out (by burning up all the fuel), the pain will help you forget a previous one (Benvolio is still trying to persuade Romeo that falling in love with another girl will help him forget his first love.)

48   **holp** helped

52   **plantain leaf** A herbal remedy for cuts and grazes (Romeo is scorning Benvolio's help).

55   **bound** Romeo feels that love has tied him up just as, in those days, people thought to be mad were tied up.

57   **God-den** Good evening (but a greeting that could be used any time after noon); also sometimes written as 'good den'.

Of limping winter treads, even such delight
Among fresh female buds shall you this night
Inherit at my house. Hear all, all see,   30
And like her most whose merit most shall be;
Which one more view of, many, mine being one –
May stand in number, though in reckoning none.
Come go with me. –
[*To* PETER, *giving a paper*] Go, sirrah, trudge about
Through fair Verona, find those persons out   35
Whose names are written there, and to them say,
My house and welcome on their pleasure stay.

                    [*Exeunt* CAPULET *and* PARIS

PETER   Find them out whose names are written here! It
is written that the shoemaker should meddle
with his yard, and the tailor with his last, the   40
fisher with his pencil, and the painter with his
nets. But I am sent to find those persons whose
names are here writ, and can never find what
names the writing person hath here writ. I must
to the learned, in good time.   45

Enter BENVOLIO *and* ROMEO

BENVOLIO   Tut man, one fire burns out another's burning,
One pain is lessened by another's anguish;
Turn giddy, and be holp by backward turning;
One desperate grief cures with another's languish.
Take thou some new infection to thy eye,   50
And the rank poison of the old will die.

ROMEO   Your plantain leaf is excellent for that.

BENVOLIO   For what I pray thee?

ROMEO   For your broken shin.

BENVOLIO   Why Romeo, art thou mad?

ROMEO   Not mad, but bound more than a madman is;   55
Shut up in prison, kept without my food,
Whipped and tormented, and – God-den good fellow.

PETER   God gi' god-den. I pray, sir, can you read?

Benvolio and Romeo meet the servant, who asks them to read the list for him. Romeo reads it aloud. It includes the name of Rosaline, with whom he is in love. He asks where the feast will take place .The servant tells them that the feast is at the Capulets' house. Benvolio tells Romeo that he should attend. Then he will be able to compare Rosaline, whom he loves, with other more beautiful girls and realise his mistake.

58–83 This section is in **prose**, the language of everyday conversation, suitable for Peter's enquiry.

59 **Ay … fortune** I can foresee ('read') my future in my present unhappiness. Romeo is making a pun on two meanings of 'read': 1) to predict 2) to interpret written language.

60 **Perhaps … book** Maybe you didn't need a book for that

63 **rest you merry** thank you and goodbye

73 **assembly** group of people

Whither To what place

82 **crush** drink

84–103 The rest of the scene is in **verse**, more suitable than prose for the subject matter of love. From line 88 it is rhymed, too.

84 **ancient** long-established

85 **the fair Rosaline** Clearly Romeo has told Benvolio her name after all.

87 **Go thither** Go there

with unattainted eye without prejudice

90–3 **When … liars** Heretics were people who held false beliefs and during the sixteenth century they were sometimes punished for their beliefs, and even executed by burning. Romeo sees his love as a religion. He says that when his faith accepts something so false then may his tears of love turn to fire and burn his eyes. Then, too, may people who failed the test of faith (being tied up and thrown into deep water) be burned as liars!

ROMEO	Ay, mine own fortune in my misery.
PETER	Perhaps you have learned it without book. But 60 I pray, can you read anything you see?
ROMEO	Ay, if I know the letters and the language.
PETER	Ye say honestly; rest you merry.
ROMEO	Stay fellow, I can read. [*Reads the paper* 'Signior Martino, and his wife and daughters; 65 County Anselme, and his beauteous sisters; the lady widow of Vitruvio; Signior Placentio, and his lovely nieces; Mercutio, and his brother Valentine; mine uncle Capulet, his wife, and daughters; my fair niece Rosaline, and Livia; 70 Signior Valentio, and his cousin Tybalt; Lucio, and the lively Helena.' A fair assembly. Whither should they come?
PETER	Up.
ROMEO	Whither? To supper? 75
PETER	To our house.
ROMEO	Whose house?
PETER	My master's.
ROMEO	Indeed I should have asked you that before.
PETER	Now I'll tell you without asking. My master is 80 the great rich Capulet; and if you be not of the house of Montagues, I pray come and crush a cup of wine. Rest you merry. [*Exit*
BENVOLIO	At this same ancient feast of Capulet's Sups the fair Rosaline whom thou so lov'st, 85 With all the admired beauties of Verona. Go thither, and with unattainted eye, Compare her face with some that I shall show, And I will make thee think thy swan a crow.
ROMEO	When the devout religion of mine eye 90 Maintains such falsehood, then turn tears to fire, And these who often drowned could never die, Transparent heretics, be burnt for liars.

Romeo disagrees strongly with this but says he will attend the feast to prove Benvolio wrong.

96–7   **you saw ... eye** you only thought she was beautiful because there was no one to compare her with

98   **in that ... weighed** He compares Romeo's eyes to a set of scales with which he judges (weighs) women's beauty. They are 'crystal' because they are transparent.

101   **shall ... well** won't look so good

At the Capulets' house Lady Capulet tells Juliet's Nurse to call Juliet. Juliet comes. Lady Capulet and the Nurse discuss how old Juliet is: not quite fourteen.

2   **by my ... old** The Nurse swears by her virginity, which she apparently lost at the age of 12.

3   **What** She is impatient.

   lady-bird! sweetheart!

4   **God forbid!** She hopes nothing has happened to Juliet to stop her coming.

   What Juliet! The Nurse is becoming even more impatient.

7   **give leave awhile** leave us alone for a while

9   **thou's ... counsel** you must hear what we are about to discuss

10   **a pretty age** a suitable age – old enough to be married

13   **teen** grief (But she is playing on the word 'fourteen' and regretting that she has only four teeth left.)

	One fairer than my love? The all-seeing sun	
	Ne'er saw her match since first the world begun.	95
BENVOLIO	Tut you saw her fair, none else being by,	
	Herself poised with herself in either eye.	
	But in that crystal scales let there be weighed	
	Your lady's love against some other maid	
	That I will show you shining at this feast,	100
	And she shall scant show well that now seems best.	
ROMEO	I'll go along, no such sight to be shown,	
	But to rejoice in splendour of mine own.	

[Exeunt

Scene ❸

A room in Capulet's mansion
Enter LADY CAPULET *and* NURSE

L. CAPULET	Nurse, where's my daughter? Call her forth to me.	
NURSE	Now by my maidenhood – at twelve year old –	
	I bade her come. What lamb! What lady-bird!	
	God forbid! Where's this girl? What Juliet!	

Enter JULIET

JULIET	How now? Who calls?	
NURSE	Your mother.	5
JULIET	Madam, I am here. What is your will?	
L. CAPULET	This is the matter – Nurse, give leave awhile,	
	We must talk in secret. Nurse, come back again,	
	I have remembered me, thou's hear our counsel.	
	Thou knowest my daughter's of a pretty age.	10
NURSE	Faith I can tell her age unto an hour.	
L. CAPULET	She's not fourteen.	
NURSE	I'll lay fourteen of my teeth,	
	And yet to my teen be it spoken, I have but four,	

The Nurse continues to recall events of Juliet's life when she was only two.

17	**Lammas Eve** 31st July: Lammas was a Church harvest festival held on 1st August.
19	**Susan is with God** Susan was the Nurse's own daughter. The baby had died and the Nurse was engaged to breastfeed Juliet. This was common practice in wealthy families.
22	**marry** indeed
23	**earthquake** The Nurse is dating Juliet's weaning to a day when the earth shook.
26	**wormwood to my dug** (to discourage the baby from breastfeeding.) When it was to be weaned, the nurse would use the bitter juice of a plant on her nipples.
27	**dove-house** dove-cote, where tame doves were kept for food
29	**Nay ... brain** I've got brains all right
31	**pretty fool** the poor little dear
32	**tetchy** irritable
33	**'Shake' ... dove-house** As the earth shook, so did the dove-cote and this told the Nurse to move away with the baby.
34	**trudge** move off
36	**high-lone** all by herself
	the rood Christ's cross
38	**broke her brow** (fell down and) bumped her forehead
40	**A'** He
42	**Thou ... wit** When you know a bit more, you'll fall on your back. He is making a coarse joke which the baby cannot, of course, understand.
43	**my holidame** by Our Lady
44	**Ay** Yes
45	**To see ... about!** Strange how a joke can come true!
	I warrant, an I grant, if

	She's not fourteen. How long is it now	
	To Lammas-tide?	
L. CAPULET	A fortnight and odd days.	15
NURSE	Even or odd, of all days in the year,	

come Lammas Eve at night shall she be fourteen.
Susan and she – God rest all Christian souls –
Were of an age. Well, Susan is with God,
She was too good for me. But as I said,   20
On Lammas Eve at night shall she be fourteen;
That shall she, marry, I remember it well.
'Tis since the earthquake now eleven years,
and she was weaned – I never shall forget it –
Of all the days of the year, upon that day.   25
For I had then laid wormwood to my dug,
Sitting in the sun under the dove-house wall.
My lord and you were then at Mantua –
Nay I do bear a brain – but as I said,
When it did taste the wormwood on the nipple   30
Of my dug, and felt it bitter, pretty fool,
To see it tetchy, and fall out with the dug.
'Shake', quoth the dove-house; 'twas no need, I
      trow,
To bid me trudge.
And since that time it is eleven years,   35
For then she could stand high-lone; nay by the rood,
She could have run and waddled all about;
For even the day before, she broke her brow,
And then my husband – God be with his soul,
A' was a merry man – took up the child.   40
'Yea,' quoth he, 'dost thou fall upon thy face?
Thou wilt fall backward when thou hast more wit,
Wilt thou not Jule?' And by my holidame,
The pretty wretch left crying, and said 'Ay'.
To see how a jest shall come about! I warrant, an   45
I should live a thousand years,
I should never forget it. 'Wilt thou not Jule?'
      quoth he,

Lady Capulet stops her, to ask Juliet how she would feel about the prospect of getting married. Lady Capulet reveals that Juliet has a suitor, Count Paris.

48   **pretty ... stinted** the little dear stopped (crying)

49   **I prithee ... peace** please stop talking

52–3 **I warrant ... stone** I guarantee it had on its forehead a bump as big as a young cock's testicle

54   **A perilous knock** A dreadful blow

57   **stinted** stopped

58   **And stint ... say I** Please, Nurse, will you stop too, I beg you

59   **God ... grace** May God grant you his grace

61   **And I ... once** If I could only live to see you married

67–8 **Were ... teat** If it weren't for the fact that I was the only nurse to feed you, I would say you took in your wisdom with the milk when you fed

70   **ladies of esteem** ladies from good families

72   **much ... years** at about the same age

74   **The valiant ... love** the brave Count Paris is asking for your hand in marriage

76   **a man of wax** like a waxwork, perfect

80   **behold** see

	And pretty fool it stinted, and said 'Ay'.	
L. CAPULET	Enough of this, I prithee hold thy peace.	
NURSE	Yes madam, yet I cannot choose but laugh,	50
	To think it should leave crying and say 'Ay'.	
	And yet I warrant it had upon it brow	
	A bump as big as a young cockerel's stone.	
	A perilous knock, and it cried bitterly.	
	'Yea' quoth my husband, 'fall'st upon thy face?	55
	Thou wilt fall backward when thou comest to age;	
	Wilt thou not Jule?' It stinted, and said 'Ay'.	
JULIET	And stint thou too, I pray thee, Nurse, say I.	
NURSE	Peace, I have done. God mark thee to his grace;	
	Thou wast the prettiest babe that e'er I nursed.	60
	And I might live to see thee married once,	
	I have my wish.	
L. CAPULET	Marry, that 'marry' is the very theme	
	I came to talk of. Tell me daughter Juliet,	
	How stands your dispositions to be married?	65
JULIET	It is an honour that I dream not of.	
NURSE	An honour? Were not I thine only nurse,	
	I would say thou hadst sucked wisdom from thy	
	tcat.	
L. CAPULET	Well, think of marriage now. Younger than you,	
	Here in Verona, ladies of esteem,	70
	Are made already mothers. By my count,	
	I was your mother much upon these years	
	That you are now a maid. Thus then in brief	
	The valiant Paris seeks you for his love.	
NURSE	A man, young lady; lady, such a man	75
	As all the world – why, he's a man of wax.	
L. CAPULET	Verona's summer hath not such a flower.	
NURSE	Nay he's a flower, in faith, a very flower.	
L. CAPULET	What say you, can you love the gentleman?	
	This night you shall behold him at our feast.	80

Lady Capulet urges Juliet to meet Paris at the feast they are holding that night. Juliet says she will do so. They prepare to go to the feast.

81 **volume** Lady Capulet compares Paris to a book that Juliet should read. This comparison is continued over several lines (an **extended image** – see Glossary p. 289).

82 **writ** written

83 **married lineament** harmonious feature

84 **one ... content** they all fit together so perfectly

85–6 **what ... eyes** find the things that are hidden in the main part of the book written in the margin (of his eyes)

87 **this unbound lover** A **play on words**: he is like a book that is incomplete, without a cover, and he is also, as a lover, free to do as he likes, because he is not married.

89–92 **The fish ... story** These two sentences go together. Lady Capulet describes Paris as the contents ('golden story') of the book and Juliet as the cover ('gold clasps'). Just as the sea provides a home for the fish that live in it, so the handsome cover (Juliet) will provide a perfect home for the book (Paris).

95 **women grow by men** A **play on words**: by marriage women grow in status, but they also grow in size by becoming pregnant.

97 **look ... move** I'll look forward to liking him, if looking at him can lead me to like him

98–9 **But ... fly** But I won't allow my eye to get me more involved (with him) than you would approve of

102–3 **in extremity** is urgent

104 **straight** immediately

106 **stays** is waiting

Read o'er the volume of young Paris' face,
And find delight writ there with beauty's pen;
Examine every married lineament,
And see how one another lends content;
And what obscured in this fair volume lies   85
Find written in the margent of his eyes.
This precious book of love, this unbound lover,
To beautify him only lacks a cover.
The fish lives in the sea, and 'tis much pride
For fair without the fair within to hide.   90
That book in many's eyes doth share the glory,
That in gold clasps locks in the golden story.
So shall you share all that he doth possess,
By having him, making yourself no less.

NURSE   No less, nay bigger; women grow by men.   95

L. CAPULET Speak briefly; can you like of Paris' love?

JULIET   I'll look to like, if looking liking move.
But no more deep will I endart mine eye
Than your consent gives strength to make it fly.

Enter PETER *the Clown*

PETER   Madam, the guests are come, supper served up,   100
you called, my young lady asked for, the Nurse
cursed in the pantry, and every thing in
extremity. I must hence to wait; I beseech you
follow straight.

L. CAPULET We follow thee. [*Exit* PETER] Juliet, the County   105
stays.

NURSE   Go girl, seek happy nights to happy days

[*Exeunt*

Act 1 scenes 2 and 3

Meet the family

In Act 1 scene 1 we met Romeo's parents and heard them describing their concern about his behaviour. In scenes 2 and 3 we meet first Juliet's father and then her mother and Nurse. They are all very excited that a wealthy young man, Paris, is seeking Juliet's hand in marriage. How they react tells us a lot about them individually, as family members.

Capulet

1   In the table below, key sections of text from Act 1 scene 2 have been picked out. You can use the table to develop ideas about what sort of father Capulet is. Copy it and fill in the blanks. Some of them have been started for you.

	Lines	What they mean	What they tell us about him
Capulet	10–13	Paris wants to marry soon. Capulet says he should wait: Juliet is too young.	He is a caring father who wants his daughter to be happy.
	14	All his other children have died.	
	18–19		

What sort of father is Capulet?

He seems to care a lot about his daughter...

Lady Capulet

2   Now make a similar table for Lady Capulet. Comment on these lines from Act 1 scene 3: 69–71, 73–4, 79, and 96.

Juliet

3   Now make a similar table for Juliet. Comment on these lines from Act 1 scene 3: 66, and 97–9.

Performance: the Nurse

The Nurse is a character who talks a lot. She is usually presented as a comic character. Much of the humour comes from that fact that she doesn't realise what other people think about her.

Work on your own

1 Read lines 16–58 from Act 1 scene 3 carefully and make detailed notes on how you think Lady Capulet and Juliet might react to the Nurse. Set out your notes in a table like this:

Lines	Lady Capulet	Juliet
16–19	Lady Capulet sighs and sits down heavily. She knows they can't stop the Nurse for a while.	Juliet raises her eyes to her mother to show she knows the Nurse is 'going off on one'.

Work in a group of three or four

2 Compare notes with the other members of the group. Discuss which is the best interpretation of the reactions of the two characters.

3 Cast the three parts. If there are four in the group, the fourth person should act as director.

4 Act out the lines, making them as amusing as possible. Pay special attention to how Juliet and her mother respond to what the Nurse says.

Marriage is...

The main topic of conversation in these two scenes is marriage. Different characters have different attitudes towards marriage. Look back through the scenes at what each of these characters says about marriage: Capulet, Lady Capulet, Nurse, and Juliet

Now write one sentence for each character summing up what they think. Begin each sentence: 'Marriage is...'

Quotation quiz

For each of these quotations, work out:

1 who said it

2 who they were speaking to

3 what it tells us about

 a the speaker

 b any other characters.

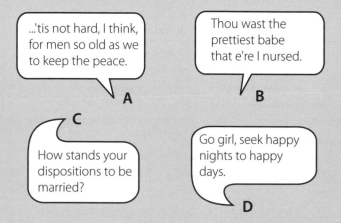

...'tis not hard, I think, for men so old as we to keep the peace.

A

Thou wast the prettiest babe that e're I nursed.

B

C

How stands your dispositions to be married?

Go girl, seek happy nights to happy days.

D

Romeo, Mercutio, Benvolio, and their friends are on their way to the Capulets' ball.

1 **What ... excuse?** Romeo asks whether they need to make a formal speech to explain their arrival, uninvited.

2 **on** continue

3 **The date ... prolixity** Such formal wordy speeches are out of date

4 **Cupid ... scarf** the guest presenting the group of maskers could represent Cupid, blindfolded, and carrying an imitation bow and arrows

E At this same ancient feast of Capulet's Sups the fair Rosaline whom thou so lov'st...

F Younger than she are happy mothers made.

G Take thou some new infection to thy eye, And the rank poison of the old will die.

H Earth hath swallowed all my hopes but she, She is the hopeful lady of my earth.

I I must to the learned, in good time.

J I'll look to like if looking liking move. But no more deep will I endart mine eye Than your consent gives strength to make it fly.

Scene ④

A street outside Capulet's mansion
Enter ROMEO, MERCUTIO, *and* BENVOLIO *with other Maskers and Torch-bearers*

ROMEO   What, shall this speech be spoke for our excuse?
         Or shall we on without apology?

BENVOLIO   The date is out of such prolixity.
         We'll have no Cupid hoodwinked with a scarf,

Romeo is gloomy, partly because he is unhappily in love and because he is worried about how they will explain themselves: they haven't got invitations. Benvolio and Mercutio try to cheer him up, but with little success.

5	**Bearing ... lath** the bow would be made of painted wood and shaped like the one you see in paintings of Cupid
6	**crow-keeper** scarecrow
7	**without-book prologue** an introductory speech, supposed to have been learnt by heart
9	**But ... will** They must judge us by whatever standard they choose
10	**We'll ... be gone** we will pace out a dance and go: these are **puns** on the various meanings of 'measure'.
12	**Being ... light** Romeo is in a dark mood and so offers to carry the light – the torch. The torch-bearer would not dance.
15	**nimble ... lead** Romeo describes the soles of his friends' shoes as smooth and swift for dancing and compares them with his heavy spirit – a play on the words 'sole'/'soul'.
18	**common bound** ordinary leap in dancing (with a reference to 'tied up' and 'bound' meaning 'boundary')
19	**empierced ... shaft** pierced through with his arrow
20–1	**so bound ... dull** woe so tied down I cannot leap higher than this dull misery
24	**Too ... thing** too heavy for such a delicate thing
28	**Prick ... down** Treat love as you say it is treating you and you will beat it
29	**a case ... visage in** a mask for my face
30	**A visor for a visor** A mask for a face
30–1	**What ... deformities?** Why should I care if people notice that I am not handsome, since a mask will cover my face?
32	**beetle brows** heavy eyebrows
34	**betake ... legs** start dancing
35	**wantons** frivolous people
36	**Tickle ... heels** dance on the rushes (a temporary floor covering) which have no feeling
37	**I am ... phrase** I have an old proverb in mind

	Bearing a Tartar's painted bow of lath,	5
	Scaring the ladies like a crow-keeper;	
	Nor no without-book prologue, faintly spoke	
	After the prompter, for our entrance.	
	But let them measure us by what they will,	
	We'll measure them a measure, and be gone.	10

ROMEO   Give me a torch, I am not for this ambling.
             Being but heavy, I will bear the light.

MERCUTIO   Nay, gentle Romeo, we must have you dance.

ROMEO   Not I, believe me, you have dancing shoes
             With nimble soles, I have a soul of lead   15
             So stakes me to the ground I cannot move.

MERCUTIO   You are a lover; borrow Cupid's wings,
             And soar with them above a common bound.

ROMEO   I am too sore empierced with his shaft,
             To soar with his light feathers; and so bound,   20
             I cannot bound a pitch above dull woe.
             Under love's heavy burden do I sink.

MERCUTIO   And to sink in it should you burden love;
             Too great oppression for a tender thing.

ROMEO   Is love a tender thing? It is too rough,   25
             Too rude, too boisterous, and it pricks like thorn.

MERCUTIO   If love be rough with you, be rough with love.
             Prick love for pricking, and you beat love down.
             Give me a case to put my visage in.
             A visor for a visor. What care I   30
             What curious eye doth quote deformities?
             Here are the beetle brows shall blush for me.

BENVOLIO   Come knock and enter, and no sooner in,
             But every man betake him to his legs.

ROMEO   A torch for me; let wantons light of heart   35
             Tickle the senseless rushes with their heels.
             For I am proverbed with a grandsire phrase:
             I'll be a candle-holder and look on;
             The game was ne'er so fair, and I am done.

Mercutio continues to try to joke Romeo out of his sombre mood. When Romeo mentions a dream, Mercutio launches into a fanciful account of Queen Mab who travels into people's dreams.

40   **dun's the mouse** Mercutio makes a pun on 'done', saying 'dun' (brown) is a quiet and boring mouselike colour. Scholars are not sure about the reference to 'constable'.

41   **If thou ... mire** On the other hand, if you're a horse called Dun we'll pull you out of the mud. This refers to a boisterous game where a log named Dun would be thrown into a room and the players would rush to get it out, pushing the others aside. As a proverb it means 'to lend a helping hand to someone in distress'.

42   **Of this ... love** of this thing called 'love' (His friends want to rescue Romeo from the state he has got himself into.)

43   **we burn daylight** we are wasting time

45   **We waste ... day** the waste here is like burning torches in daylight

46–7 **for our ... wits** reason is more reliable than anything our five senses can tell us

49   **'tis no wit to go** it is not wise to go

51   **lie** 'Lie' can mean 'lie in bed' or 'tell lies'.

53   **Queen Mab** the queen of the fairies

54   **the fairies' midwife** Just as a midwife helps deliver babies, so Queen Mab helps deliver dreams.

55   **agate** A precious stone used in signet rings, often engraved with a tiny picture.

56   **alderman** a senior local councillor

57   **atomies** atoms

59   **spinners** craneflies (or daddy-long-legs)

61   **traces** the straps that connect the horse's harness to the wagon

62   **collars** the horses' collars

65–6 **a round ... maid** People used to say that maggots would breed in the hands of girls who were lazy.

68   **joiner** Someone who works in wood, making windows, doors, etc.

MERCUTIO	Tut, dun's the mouse, the constable's own word. 40
	If thou art Dun, we'll draw thee from the mire
	Of this save-your-reverence love, wherein thou
	stickest
	Up to the ears. Come, we burn daylight, ho!
ROMEO	Nay that's not so.
MERCUTIO	I mean sir, in delay
	We waste our lights in vain, like lights by day. 45
	Take our good meaning, for our judgement sits
	Five times in that, ere once in our five wits.
ROMEO	And we mean well in going to this mask;
	But 'tis no wit to go.
MERCUTIO	Why, may one ask?
ROMEO	I dreamt a dream tonight.
MERCUTIO	And so did I. 50
ROMEO	Well, what was yours?
MERCUTIO	That dreamers often lie.
ROMEO	In bed asleep while they do dream things true.
MERCUTIO	O then I see Queen Mab hath been with you.
	She is the fairies' midwife, and she comes
	In shape no bigger than an agate stone 55
	On the fore-finger of an alderman,
	Drawn with a team of little atomies
	Over men's noses as they lie asleep.
	Her wagon-spokes made of long spinners' legs;
	The cover, of the wings of grasshoppers; 60
	Her traces, of the smallest spider web;
	Her collars, of the moonshine's watery beams;
	Her whip, of cricket's bone; the lash, of film;
	Her wagoner, a small grey-coated gnat,
	Not half so big as a round little worm 65
	Pricked from the lazy finger of a maid.
	Her chariot is an empty hazel-nut,
	Made by the joiner squirrel or old grub,
	Time out a mind the fairies' coachmakers.

Mercutio describes how Queen Mab leads people to dream of what they most desire – although this only shows their least attractive side.

72   **courtiers** People who spent time at the royal court, often trying to gain money, titles or power for themselves.

       curtsies Courtiers would have to show 'courtesies', marks of politeness, to the king or queen when at court.

73   **straight** immediately

76   **sweetmeats** eaten to make the breath smell sweet

78   **smelling out a suit** Courtiers made money by offering to put in a good word to the king or queen for someone who wanted a favour.

79   **tithe-pig** The parson was entitled to one tenth (a tithe) of the income of everyone in the parish. So if your sow had a litter, the tenth piglet had to go to the parson.

80   **parson** parish priest

81   **benefice** the parson's living – the parish and the income he got from it

84–5   **Of breaches ... deep** of breaking down castle walls, of ambushes, of Spanish swords (the best), of drinks thirty feet deep

90   **bakes ... hairs** makes dirty hair into matted tangles

92–4   **This ... carriage** People believed that if someone dreamed about lovemaking, the partner they dreamed of was really a devil or evil fairy.

98   **Begot** born

       vain useless

99   **Which ... air** it is not solid

100   **inconstant** changeable

100–1   **woos ... north** The wind is compared to a lover, altering his affection from one woman to another.

And in this state she gallops night by night   70
Through lovers' brains, and then they dream of
      love;
O'er courtiers' knees, that dream on curtsies
      straight;
O'er lawyers' fingers, who straight dream on fees;
O'er ladies' lips, who straight on kisses dream,
Which oft the angry Mab with blisters plagues,   75
Because their breaths with sweetmeats tainted are.
Sometime she gallops o'er a courtier's nose,
And then dreams he of smelling out a suit;
And sometime comes she with a tithe-pig's tail,
Tickling a parson's nose as 'a lies asleep,   80
Then dreams he of another benefice.
Sometime she driveth o'er a soldier's neck,
And then dreams he of cutting foreign throats,
Of breaches, ambuscadoes, Spanish blades,
Of healths five fathom deep; and then anon   85
Drums in his ear, at which he starts and wakes;
And being thus frighted, swears a prayer or two,
And sleeps again. This is that very Mab
That plaits the manes of horses in the night,
And bakes the elf-locks in foul sluttish hairs,   90
Which once untangled much misfortune bodes.
This is the hag, when maids lie on their backs,
That presses them and learns them first to bear,
Making them women of good carriage.
This is she –

ROMEO   Peace, peace, Mercutio, peace.   95
Thou talk'st of nothing.

MERCUTIO   True, I talk of dreams;
Which are the children of an idle brain,
Begot of nothing but vain fantasy;
Which is as thin of substance as the air,
And more inconstant than the wind who woos   100
Even now the frozen bosom of the north,
And being angered puffs away from thence,

Benvolio points out that they are just wasting time. Romeo speaks of his sense of foreboding about what is to happen. They move on to the Capulets' house, where dinner is over and the servants are preparing for the masked dance.

103   **south** Just as the north wind is bitterly cold, the south wind is warmer and likely to produce dew or rain.

104   **blows ... ourselves** is stopping us from getting on

106   **my mind misgives** I have a premonition

107–11 Some ... death Romeo believes that he has mortgaged his life in return for love. It is written in the stars that events that night will lead to his being asked to repay this debt with his life.

114   **Strike, drum** Benvolio tells the one carrying the drum to beat it.

The servants rush around, clearing up after the meal. Sampson and Gregory criticise their fellow-servants, and Sampson bosses the others around.

1–2   **Where's ... trencher?** Sampson is cross that the kitchen servants are not getting rid of the food remaining on the trenchers (wooden plates) and clearing the tables.

4   **foul** dirty

6   **joint-stools** stools made by a joiner

6–7   **court-cupboard** sideboard

7   **plate** silver or gold dishes and other items

8   **marchpane** marzipan

14–15 Cheerly ... all Potpan tries to get them all to hurry up, using a proverb with the sense of 'hang in there, and you'll get through'.

Turning his side to the dew-dropping south.

BENVOLIO   This wind you talk of blows us from ourselves.
Supper is done, and we shall come too late.   105

ROMEO   I fear, too early; for my mind misgives
Some consequence, yet hanging in the stars,
Shall bitterly begin his fearful date
With this night's revels, and expire the term
Of a despised life closed in my breast,   110
By some vile forfeit of untimely death.
But he that hath the steerage of my course
Direct my suit. On lusty gentlemen.

BENVOLIO   Strike, drum.

Scene ❺

The Great Hall in Capulet's mansion
They march about the stage, and the Servingmen
come forth with napkins

SAMPSON   Where's Potpan, that he helps not to take away?
He shift a trencher? He scrape a trencher?

GREGORY   When good manners shall lie all in one or two
men's hands, and they unwashed too, 'tis a foul
thing.   5

SAMPSON   Away with the joint-stools, remove the court-
cupboard, look to the plate. Good thou, save me
a piece of marchpane, and as thou lovest me, let
the porter let in Susan Grindstone and Nell.
Anthony and Potpan!   10

ANTHONY   Ay boy, ready.

SAMPSON   You are looked for, and called for, asked for, and
sought for in the great chamber.

POTPAN   We cannot be here and there too. Cheerly boys,
be brisk awhile, and the longer liver take all.   15

Capulet welcomes his guests to the ball and encourages them to dance. Some of the ladies are a bit shy and Capulet teases them that if they don't dance people will think they've got corns on their feet. He tells the musicians to play and the servants to clear the tables out of the way. Then he and an elderly relative sit watching the dancers and reminisce about the last time the two of them danced like this. Romeo catches sight of Juliet.

17	**Unplagued** untroubled
	walk a bout have a dance
19	**makes dainty** is shy
20	**Am I ... now?** Have I got to the truth of it now?
22	**visor** mask
26	**A hall, a hall** Clear a space for the dance
27	**turn the tables up** move the tables out of the way
29	**unlooked-for** unexpected
33	**By'r lady** He swears by the Virgin Mary.
35	**nuptial** wedding
36	**Pentecost** the Christian festival of Whitsun, 50 days after Easter; Whitsun commemerates the descent of the Holy Spirit on the disciples of Jesus Christ.
40	**but a ward** not yet an adult
41–2	**which doth ... knight** who is dancing with that nobleman

Enter CAPULET, LADY CAPULET, JULIET, TYBALT,
and all the Guests and Gentlewomen to the Maskers

CAPULET Welcome gentlemen. Ladies that have their toes
Unplagued with corns will walk a bout with you.
Ah ha, my mistresses, which of you all
Will now deny to dance? She that makes dainty,
She I'll swear hath corns. Am I come near ye now? 20
Welcome gentlemen. I have seen the day
That I have worn a visor and could tell
A whispering tale in a fair lady's ear,
Such as would please. 'Tis gone, 'tis gone, 'tis gone.
You are welcome, gentlemen. Come, musicians
        play. 25
A hall, a hall, give room, and foot it girls.

                    [*Music plays, and they dance*

More light you knaves, and turn the tables up;
And quench the fire, the room is grown too hot.
Ah sirrah, this unlooked-for sport comes well.
Nay sit, nay sit, good cousin Capulet, 30
For you and I are past our dancing days.
How long is't now since last yourself and I
Were in a mask?

2ND CAPULET   By'r lady, thirty years.

CAPULET What man, 'tis not so much, 'tis not so much.
'Tis since the nuptial of Lucentio, 35
Come Pentecost as quickly as it will,
Some five and twenty years, and then we
        masked.

2ND CAPULET 'Tis more, 'tis more, his son is elder sir;
His son is thirty.

CAPULET   Will you tell me that?
His son was but a ward two years ago. 40

ROMEO [*To a* SERVINGMAN] What lady's that which doth
        enrich the hand
Of yonder knight?

SERVINGMAN   I know not sir.

Romeo is stunned by Juliet's beauty. Tybalt sees Romeo and recognises him as a Montague. He becomes very angry but Capulet orders him to do nothing.

45   **Ethiop** a black African

47–50 **So shows ... hand** That lady stands out from the others like a white dove among black crows. When the dance is over, I'll watch where she goes and then, by touching her hand, bless my own rough hand

51   **Forswear** Deny

54   **Fetch ... boy** Tybalt tells his page to get his sword.

      slave a term of abuse

55   **antic face** weird mask

56   **fleer** make fun

      solemnity festivities

57   **by the ... kin** by the ancestors and honour of my family

65   **'A bears ... gentleman** He behaves himself like a well-mannered person from a good family

67   **well governed** well-behaved

69   **do him disparagement** insult him

70   **take no note** leave him alone

71–3 **It is ... feast** this is what I want and if you respect me you will put a good face on things and not scowl, because such behaviour is totally unsuitable for a celebration

74   **It fits** It is suitable

75   **endure** put up with

ROMEO	O she doth teach the torches to burn bright.
	It seems she hangs upon the cheek of night
	Like a rich jewel in an Ethiop's ear; 45
	Beauty too rich for use, for earth too dear.
	So shows a snowy dove trooping with crows,
	As yonder lady o'er her fellows shows.
	The measure done, I'll watch her place of stand,
	And, touching hers make blessed my rude hand. 50
	Did my heart love till now? Forswear it sight,
	For I ne'er saw true beauty till this night.
TYBALT	This by his voice should be a Montague.
	Fetch me my rapier, boy. What dares the slave
	Come hither, covered with an antic face, 55
	To fleer and scorn at our solemnity?
	Now by the stock and honour of my kin,
	To strike him dead I hold it not a sin.
CAPULET	Why how now kinsman, wherefore storm you so?
TYBALT	Uncle, this is a Montague, our foe; 60
	A villain that is hither come in spite,
	To scorn at our solemnity this night.
CAPULET	Young Romeo is it?
TYBALT	'Tis he, that villain Romeo.
CAPULET	Content thee gentle coz, let him alone.
	'A bears him like a portly gentleman; 65
	And to say truth, Verona brags of him
	To be a virtuous and well-governed youth.
	I would not for the wealth of all this town
	Here in my house do him disparagement.
	Therefore be patient, take no note of him; 70
	It is my will, the which if thou respect,
	Show a fair presence, and put off these frowns,
	An ill-beseeming semblance for a feast.
TYBALT	It fits when such a villain is a guest.
	I'll not endure him.
CAPULET	He shall be endured. 75

67

Tybalt protests but Capulet is firm. Tybalt leaves, muttering that he will not forget what has happened. Romeo approaches Juliet and speaks to her for the first time.

76 **goodman boy** A deliberate insult, putting Tybalt in his place.

Go to An expression of anger.

78 **God shall ... soul** Bless me!

79–80 **You'll ... man** You want to cause a disturbance amongst my guests? You want to stir it all up? You'd be a really big boy then, wouldn't you?

82 **saucy** insolent (stronger in Shakespeare's day)

83 **This ... scathe you** If you go on like this, you'll suffer for it

84 **contrary** contradict

85 **princox** insolent boy

88–91 **Patience ... gall** I'm forced to be patient, but inside I'm boiling with rage and this mixture of feelings makes me tremble. I'll go away (and calm down) but although my mood may seem sweet now, it will turn into bitter hatred

92–109 **If I ... book** These lines contain a group of images about religion. People still believed that especially holy people ('saints') could perform miracles. When a saint died and was buried, their 'shrine' was visited by 'pilgrims' (or 'palmers') who often 'prayed' for miracles, or that their 'sins' could be forgiven ('purged'). The saint's shrine was a very holy place and pilgrims had to treat it with reverence and make sure that they did not defile ('profane') it. Romeo speaks of Juliet's hand as the shrine to which pilgrims (his lips) travel to worship (kiss). Even touching the shrine may defile it, but then his lips will remedy this. Lines 92–105 are in the form of a **sonnet** (see p. 14).

97 **mannerly** well-behaved

99 **palm to palm ... kiss** Pilgrims returning from the Holy Land carried a palm and so were called palmers. A more suitable greeting ('kiss') for a palmer would be to touch hands ('palms').

104 **Saints do not move** Juliet is thinking of the statue of the saint at the shrine.

	What goodman boy, I say he shall; Go to,	
	Am I the master here or you? Go to.	
	You'll not endure him? God shall mend my soul,	
	You'll make a mutiny among my guests?	
	You will set cock-a-hoop, you'll be the man?	80
TYBALT	Why, uncle, 'tis a shame –	
CAPULET	Go to, go to,	
	You are a saucy boy. Is't so indeed?	
	This trick may chance to scathe you I know what.	
	You must contrary me? Marry 'tis time.	
	[*To Guests*] Well said my hearts! [*To* TYBALT] You are a princox, go;	85
	Be quiet, or – [*To Servants*] More light, more light! [*To* TYBALT] For shame!	
	I'll make you quiet. [*To Guests*] What, cheerly my hearts!	
TYBALT	Patience perforce with wilful choler meeting	
	Makes my flesh tremble in their different greeting.	
	I will withdraw, but this intrusion shall,	90
	Now seeming sweet, convert to bitterest gall.	
	[*Exit*	
ROMEO	[*To* JULIET] If I profane with my unworthiest hand	
	This holy shrine, the gentle sin is this,	
	My lips two blushing pilgrims ready stand	
	To smooth that rough touch with a tender kiss.	95
JULIET	Good pilgrim, you do wrong your hand too much,	
	Which mannerly devotion shows in this;	
	For saints have hands that pilgrims' hands do touch,	
	And palm to palm is holy palmers' kiss.	
ROMEO	Have not saints lips, and holy palmers too?	100
JULIET	Ay pilgrim lips that they must use in prayer.	
ROMEO	O then dear saint, let lips do what hands do.	
	They pray; grant thou, lest faith turn to despair.	
JULIET	Saints do not move, though grant for prayers' sake.	

They kiss. The Nurse interrupts with a message that Juliet's mother wishes to speak to her. Romeo asks the Nurse who Juliet is and learns that she is a Capulet. The guests begin to leave.

105   **prayer's effect** the kiss

106   **purged** cleansed

108   **O trespass sweetly urged** He says that she is persuading him to 'sin' (kiss her) again.

109   **by th' book** expertly

116   **have the chinks** get the cash, be in the money

117   **my life ... debt** my life now depends on my enemy

118   **Away ... best** Let's leave now while things are still going really well

119   **Ay ... unrest** Romeo agrees; things have gone 'well' for him, but he is dismayed at what will happen in the future because of his new love for Juliet.

121   **banquet** light refreshments

SD   ***They whisper*** The guests excuse themselves. We have to guess what they say, from Capulet's reply.

125   **fay** faith

          waxes grows

127   **yond** over there

ROMEO	Then move not, while my prayer's effect I take. 105
	[*Kisses her*
	Thus from my lips, by thine, my sin is purged.
JULIET	Then have my lips the sin that they have took.
ROMEO	Sin from my lips? O trespass sweetly urged.
	Give me my sin again.
JULIET	You kiss by th' book.
NURSE	Madam your mother craves a word with you. 110
ROMEO	What is her mother?
NURSE	Marry bachelor,
	Her mother is the lady of the house,
	And a good lady, and a wise and virtuous.
	I nursed her daughter that you talked withal.
	I tell you, he that can lay hold of her 115
	Shall have the chinks.
ROMEO	Is she a Capulet?
	O dear account, my life is my foe's debt.
BENVOLIO	Away, be gone, the sport is at the best.
ROMEO	Ay, so I fear, the more is my unrest.
CAPULET	Nay gentleman, prepare not to be gone; 120
	We have a trifling foolish banquet towards.
	[*They whisper in his ear*
	Is it e'en so? Why then I thank you all.
	I thank you honest gentlemen; good night.
	More torches here! Come on then, let's to bed.
	Ah sirrah, by my fay, it waxes late. 125
	I'll to my rest.
	[*Exeunt*
JULIET	Come hither Nurse. What is yond gentleman?
NURSE	The son and heir of old Tiberio.
JULIET	What's he that now is going out of door?
NURSE	Marry that I think be young Petruchio. 130
JULIET	What's he that follows here that would not dance?
	[*Exit* ROMEO

Juliet sends her Nurse to discover Romeo's name. She is dismayed to learn that he is a Montague. Then they, too, leave.

134	**My ... wedding-bed** I'll die unmarried (or I'll die if I can't marry him)
138	**Too ... late!** I saw Romeo and fell in love with him before I knew who he was. Now I do know who he is, it's too late for me to change my feelings!
139	**Prodigious** Monstrous
142	**withal** recently

ACTIVITIES

Act 1 scenes 4 and 5

Boys' talk

Act 1 scene 4 shows Benvolio, Mercutio, Romeo, and their friends on the way to the Capulets' party. Each of the main three characters has a different attitude towards the party. Romeo and Mercutio seem to have very different ideas about love.

Work on your own

1   Read lines 11–39 and 95–114 and think about the different 'voices' you hear as you read.

Work with a partner

2   Discuss your first impressions of Benvolio, Mercutio, and Romeo.

NURSE	I know not.
JULIET	Go ask his name – If he be married, My grave is like to be my wedding-bed.
NURSE	His name is Romeo, and a Montague, 135 The only son of your great enemy.
JULIET	My only love sprung from my only hate, Too early seen unknown, and known too late! Prodigious birth of love it is to me, That I must love a loathed enemy. 140
NURSE	What 's tis, what 's tis?
JULIET	A rhyme I learned even now Of one I danced withal. [*One calls within 'Juliet!'*]
NURSE	Anon, anon! Come let's away, the strangers all are gone.

[*Exeunt*

3 Now sum up your ideas as a series of points. For each one find
   evidence to back up your ideas. Use a table like the one below,
   which has been started for you.

Character	Point	Evidence	Explanation
Romeo	• He doesn't feel like going to the party. •	• 'I am not for this ambling' •	• He's deliberately rude about dancing ('ambling') •
Mercutio	• He tries to persuade Romeo to join in. •	• 'Nay gentle Romeo, we must have you dance.' •	• •
Benvolio			

73

Work in a group of four

4   Using lines 11–39 and 95–114 cast the parts of Romeo, Mercutio, and Benvolio. The fourth person acts as director.

5   Look at the tables you have made up and discuss how to convey these ideas when you act the scene.

6   Rehearse the scene.

7   When you have finished, discuss how far it gets across your ideas about the characters. If necessary, try it again with changes.

Storyboard

Act 1 scene 5 is a big scene with a lot of characters and a wide variety of actions. Imagine that you have been asked to direct the scene. You decide to prepare for rehearsal by producing a storyboard.

Work on your own

1   Divide the scene into sections and write down the line numbers of your sections.

2   Make a storyboard for the scene, following the pattern below. For each section:

    a   write the characters who are active in that section. If there are other characters around who do not do or say anything, leave them out

    b   describe the main actions.

Lines	Characters	Visual	Action
1–10	Gregory Sampson		Sampson and Gregory come on, shouting at each other, looking for the others.
11–15	Gregory Sampson Anthony		Anthony runs on and Sampson shouts at him. Potpan comes hurrying on from the other side.
16–26			

'What, goodman boy!'

One of the key moments in Act 1 scene 5 is the dialogue between
Capulet and Tybalt (lines 53–91):

- Capulet is the head of a wealthy family.
- Tybalt is much younger and is a junior member of the family.

You could interpret each of these characters in a number of different
ways. For example:

Capulet	Tybalt
He is now too old to control the family properly.	He doesn't respect Capulet – he thinks he's a bumbling old fool. But on an occasion like this he has to appear polite.
He admires Tybalt's courage. He's always had a soft spot for him.	He fears Capulet's power.

Work in a group of three or four

1 Cast the parts so that one person plays Tybalt, one plays Capulet
   and the other(s) watch and comment at the end.

2 Tybalt and Capulet each choose a prompt from the table above.
   Use your chosen prompt to guide your interpretation of the part.

3 Perform the scene.

4 When you have finished, discuss how it went.

5 Now think of one or two different prompts for each character.

6 Cast the parts with different actors for each part.

7 Tybalt and Capulet now choose different prompts to guide their
   interpretations of the part.

8 Perform the scene again.

9 Discuss the following questions:

   a How did each prompt affect how you spoke, moved, and reacted?

   b Which way of playing the lines worked better?

   c Which way made more sense?

'If I profane...'

The first meeting between Romeo and Juliet is the central moment of the play, but it takes up only 18 lines of Act 1 scene 5: lines 92–109. If a production is to succeed, these lines have to make a big impact on the audience. In rehearsal, the actors and the director will experiment with different interpretations before they hit on the right way to perform the lines.

Work with a partner

1 Read the lines aloud, without thinking about how they should be interpreted – just get the words right.

2 Now each choose one interpretation from the table below, and try the lines again.

Romeo	Juliet
Embarrassed, not sure how to express what you feel.	Amused: it's all just a party, isn't it?
Trying it on: this line worked before, why not now?	Really embarrassed: no one has ever spoken to her like this before.

3 Discuss how the scene went: did you find it convincing?

4 Talk about how you think the lines should be interpreted.

5 Now act them again using your chosen interpretation.

Quotation quiz

For each of the quotations below, work out:

1 who said it
2 who they were speaking to
3 what it tells us about:
   a the speaker
   b any other characters.

A You kiss by th' book.

B If love be rough with you, be rough with love.

C ...I talk of dreams; Which are the children of an idle brain...

D My only love sprung from my only hate...

E Supper is done, and we shall come too late.

F Am I the master here or you? Go to.

G O she doth teach the torches to burn bright.

H O then I see Queen Mab hath been with you.

I You are looked for, and called for, asked for, and sought for in the great chamber.

J This by his voice should be a Montague. Fetch me my rapier, boy.

The Chorus sums up what has happened in Act 1 and what will happen in Act 2.

1   **old ... lie** Romeo's previous affection for Rosaline is seen as a person who is at the point of death.

2   **young ... heir** Romeo's new desire longs eagerly (open-mouthed) to take over from the dying love.

3   **fair** beautiful young woman

      which ... die for whom Romeo ached and thought he would die without her

4   **matched** compared

5   **Romeo ... again** Romeo is not only in love, but he is loved too

6   **Alike ... looks** they have both fallen in love 'at first sight'

7   **his foe ... complain** his sighs are now directed at someone who is supposed to be his enemy (a Capulet)

8   **And ... hooks** Juliet must love where there is danger, as a fish is tempted by bait to its death

9–10   **Being ... swear** since he is considered an enemy he cannot get close to Juliet to declare his feelings, as lovers usually can

11–12   **And ... where** Juliet loves him as much, but as a young woman, she is not usually allowed out on her own, so she is even less able to meet him

13–14   **time ... meet** in time they will find a way to meet

14   **Temp'ring ... sweet** what seemed like impossible difficulties will contain great happiness

Romeo is on his way home, but turns back to the Capulets' house. Benvolio and Mercutio are looking for him but do not see him. Benvolio realises that Romeo has climbed the wall into the grounds of the Capulets' house.

1–2   **Can I ... out** Romeo asks whether he can force his body to move on and leave his heart behind. He tells his body to turn back towards Juliet, where his heart is.

6   **conjure** call up (like a magician)

Act Two

Outside Capulet's house
Enter CHORUS

CHORUS   Now old desire doth in his death-bed lie,
              And young affection gapes to be his heir.
              That fair for which love groaned for and would die,
              With tender Juliet matched, is now not fair.
              Now Romeo is beloved and loves again,   5
              Alike bewitched by the charm of looks;
              But to his foe supposed he must complain,
              And she steals love's sweet bait from fearful hooks.
              Being held a foe, he may not have access
              To breathe such vows as lovers use to swear;   10
              And she as much in love, her means much less
              To meet her new-beloved any where.
              But passion lends them power, time means, to
                  meet,
              Temp'ring extremities with extreme sweet.

                                                          [*Exit*

Scene ①

Enter ROMEO *alone*

ROMEO   Can I go forward when my heart is here?
              Turn back, dull earth, and find thy centre out.

              Enter BENVOLIO *and* MERCUTIO

BENVOLIO   Romeo! My cousin Romeo! Romeo!

MERCUTIO   He is wise,
              And on my life hath stolen him home to bed.

BENVOLIO   He ran this way and leapt this orchard wall.   5
              Call, good Mercutio.

MERCUTIO   Nay I'll conjure too.

Mercutio calls after Romeo various taunting and bawdy remarks, but, getting no response, he and Benvolio continue on their way home.

7   **Romeo ... Lover!** Mercutio tries out various names for Romeo that fit his mood.

         Humours! Moody!

8   **in the likeness of** sounding like

11   **my gossip Venus** Venus is the goddess of love. Here Mercutio reduces her to a chatty woman neighbour.

12   **purblind** completely blind

13   **trim** accurately, neatly

14   **When ... beggar-maid** An old ballad which tells the story of a king catching sight of a beautiful beggar-maid, deciding that she must become his queen, and marrying her.

16   **The ape is dead** Mercutio suggests that Romeo is pretending to be dead, as a performing monkey could be taught.

17   **I conjure ... eyes** Mercutio is still fooling about, using images of lust to make Romeo appear.

20   **the demesnes ... lie** the areas of a woman's body that are near her 'quivering thigh'

21   **in thy likeness** as yourself

24–7   **To raise ... spite** Mercutio continues with his fantasy of conjuring up spirits. The words used here contain many double meanings, mostly of a sexual nature.

27   **invocation** conjuring

31   **To be ... night** to have a damp and melancholy night as his companion, since he is sad

33   **mark** target

34   **medlar** A small brown fruit, a bit like a small apple. Because there is an opening at the top and the seeds are visible, young women make the same kind of jokes as young men.

38   **An open-arse ... pear** Another, ruder name for a medlar and a pear shaped like a penis.

39   **truckle-bed** A low bed on castors able to be pushed under a higher bed.

Romeo! Humours! Madman! Passion! Lover!
Appear thou in the likeness of a sigh,
Speak but one rhyme, and I am satisfied;
Cry but 'Ay me,' pronounce but 'love' and
   'dove'; 10
Speak to my gossip Venus one fair word,
One nickname for her purblind son and heir,
Young Abraham Cupid, he that shot so trim,
When King Cophetua loved the beggar-maid.
He heareth not, he stirreth not, he moveth not; 15
The ape is dead, and I must conjure him.
I conjure thee by Rosaline's bright eyes,
By her high forehead, and her scarlet lip,
By her fine foot, straight leg, and quivering thigh,
And the demesnes that there adjacent lie, 20
That in thy likeness thou appear to us.

BENVOLIO   And if he hear thee, thou wilt anger him.

MERCUTIO   This cannot anger him; 'twould anger him
To raise a spirit in his mistress' circle
Of some strange nature, letting it there stand 25
Till she had laid it and conjured it down;
That were some spite. My invocation
Is fair and honest; in his mistress' name,
I conjure only but to raise up him.

BENVOLIO   Come, he hath hid himself among these trees 30
To be consorted with the humorous night.
Blind is his love, and best befits the dark.

MERCUTIO   If love be blind, love cannot hit the mark.
Now will he sit under a medlar tree,
And wish his mistress were that kind of fruit 35
As maids call medlars, when they laugh alone,
O Romeo that she were, O that she were
An open-arse and thou a Poperin pear.
Romeo good night, I'll to my truckle-bed;
This field-bed is too cold for me to sleep. 40
Come, shall we go?

42   **means … found** has no intention of letting us find him

Benvolio and Mercutio leave. Romeo is in the garden of the Capulets' house. In the moonlight he sees Juliet at an upstairs window.

1   **jests at scars** makes fun of injuries (inflicted by being in love)

2   **But soft … breaks** Romeo sees Juliet at an upper window. She seems so bright to him that he compares her to the sun.

4   **moon** The house and garden are lit by the moon. In classical mythology Diana, the goddess of the moon, was served by virgins who wore a costume (vestal livery) that was pale in colour like the moonlight (sick and green). Romeo says that the moon is jealous of her maid Juliet because she is more beautiful. He encourages her to stop serving Diana, and so stop being a virgin and become his lover.

11   **O that … were** If only she knew that I am in love with her

13   **discourses** speaks

17   **spheres** In classical times people believed that the stars and planets were fixed in transparent spheres that moved around the earth.

18   **What … head?** How would it be if her eyes were shining in the sky and in their place in her head there were two stars?

21   **airy region** sky

BENVOLIO   Go then, for 'tis in vain
              To seek him here that means not to be found.

                                        [*Exeunt*

Scene ❷

Capulet's orchard

ROMEO   He jests at scars that never felt a wound.
              But soft, what light through yonder window breaks?
              It is the east, and Juliet is the sun.
              Arise fair sun and kill the envious moon,
              Who is already sick and pale with grief   5
              That thou her maid art far more fair than she.
              Be not her maid since she is envious.
              Her vestal livery is but sick and green,
              And none but fools do wear it; cast it off.

              JULIET *appears at the window*

              It is my lady, O it is my love.   10
              O that she knew she were.
              She speaks, yet she says nothing. What of that?
              Her eye discourses, I will answer it.
              I am too bold, 'tis not to me she speaks.
              Two of the fairest stars in all the heaven   15
              Having some business, do entreat her eyes
              To twinkle in their spheres till they return.
              What if her eyes were there, they in her head?
              The brightness of her cheek would shame those
                  stars,
              As daylight doth a lamp; her eyes in heaven   20
              Would through the airy region stream so bright
              That birds would sing, and think it were not night.
              See how she leans her cheek upon her hand.
              O that I were a glove upon that hand,
              That I might touch that cheek.

83

Juliet, thinking she is alone, speaks aloud of her love for Romeo and the problem that their family names cause them. But, she says, names are not important – it is the reality underneath that matters. To her surprise Romeo answers her and declares himself.

26–32 **O speak ... air** Romeo says that Juliet is like an angel because she is physically above him just as angels were seen by human beings on earth looking up at the sky.

29   **white upturned** looking upwards so that the whites show

33   **wherefore ... Romeo?** Why are you called Romeo (i.e. a Montague) and not some other name?

35   **be ... love** only promise to love me

39   **Thou ... Montague** You would still be the same person, even if you were not called Montague

44   **word** name

45–7 **So Romeo ... title** So Romeo would still be as perfect even if he were not called Romeo

46   **owes** owns

47   **doff** take off

50   **I'll be new baptised** I will go through the Christian ceremony of baptism again and change my name

52   **bescreened** hidden

53   **stumblest on my counsel** breaks in upon my secret thoughts (which she is saying out loud)

JULIET	Ay me!
ROMEO	She speaks. 25
	O speak again, bright angel, for thou art
	As glorious to this night, being o'er my head,
	As is a winged messenger of heaven
	Unto the white upturned, wond'ring eyes
	Of mortals that fall back to gaze on him, 30
	When he bestrides the lazy passing clouds,
	And sails upon the bosom of the air.
JULIET	O Romeo, Romeo, wherefore art thou Romeo?
	Deny thy father, and refuse thy name.
	Or if thou wilt not, be but sworn my love, 35
	And I'll no longer be a Capulet.
ROMEO	[*Aside*] Shall I hear more, or shall I speak at this?
JULIET	'Tis but thy name that is my enemy.
	Thou art thyself, though not a Montague.
	What's Montague? It is nor hand nor foot, 40
	Nor arm nor face, nor any other part
	Belonging to a man. O be some other name.
	What's in a name? That which we call a rose
	By any other word would smell as sweet.
	So Romeo would, were he not Romeo called, 45
	Retain that dear perfection which he owes
	Without that title. Romeo doff thy name,
	And for that name which is no part of thee,
	Take all myself.
ROMEO	I take thee at thy word.
	Call me but 'love', and I'll be new-baptised. 50
	Henceforth I never will be Romeo.
JULIET	What man art thou, that thus bescreened in night
	So stumblest on my counsel?
ROMEO	By a name
	I know not how to tell thee who I am.
	My name, dear saint, is hateful to myself. 55
	Because it is an enemy to thee.
	Had I it written, I would tear the word.

She asks how he got there. How did he find the way? Love gave him the means, he replies.

59   **Of ... uttering** that you have spoken

61   **thee dislike** is unpleasant to you

62   **wherefore** why

66   **o'erperch** fly over

67   **stony limits** boundary walls

68   **dares love** love dares to

71   **peril** danger

72   **look ... sweet** if you would only look favourably on me

73   **I am proof** I am protected

76   **but thou love me** unless you do love me

77–8   **My life ... love** I'd rather they killed me because of their hatred than go on living, waiting for death, without your love

81   **counsel** advice

82–4   **I am ... merchandise** I'm not a sailor but if you were living at the far side of the farthest ocean I would travel there to find you

88   **Fain ... form** I would much rather behave in a 'correct' formal way

89   **farewell compliment** goodbye to formal behaviour

91   **swearest** speak using flowery language and promises (as was fashionable among young men)

92   **perjuries** lies

JULIET	My ears have yet not drunk a hundred words
	Of thy tongue's uttering, yet I know the sound.
	Art thou not Romeo, and a Montague? 60
ROMEO	Neither, fair maid, if either thee dislike.
JULIET	How cam'st thou hither, tell me, and wherefore?
	The orchard walls are high, and hard to climb,
	And the place death, considering who thou art,
	If any of my kinsmen find thee here. 65
ROMEO	With love's light wings did I o'erperch these
	walls,
	For stony limits cannot hold love out,
	And what love can do, that dares love attempt.
	Therefore thy kinsmen are no stop to me.
JULIET	If they do see thee, they will murder thee. 70
ROMEO	Alack there lies more peril in thine eye
	Than twenty of their swords; look thou but sweet,
	And I am proof against their enmity.
JULIET	I would not for the world they saw thee here.
ROMEO	I have night's cloak to hide me from their eyes, 75
	And but thou love me, let them find me here.
	My life were better ended by their hate,
	Than death prorogued, wanting of thy love.
JULIET	By whose direction found'st thou out this place?
ROMEO	By love that first did prompt me to inquire; 80
	He lent me counsel, and I lent him eyes.
	I am no pilot, yet wert thou as far
	As that vast shore washed with the farthest sea,
	I should adventure for such merchandise.
JULIET	Thou knowest the mask of night is on my face, 85
	Else would a maiden blush bepaint my cheek,
	For that which thou hast heard me speak tonight.
	Fain would I dwell on form, fain, fain deny
	What I have spoke; but farewell compliment.
	Dost thou love me? I know thou wilt say 'Ay', 90
	And I will take thy word. Yet if thou swearest,
	Thou mayst prove false; at lovers' perjuries

Juliet asks if he loves her, as she loves him. She wants a simple answer, not one full of oaths. She is worried that Romeo will think she is too 'forward'. Then she says she must go.

93	**Jove** king of the gods (Roman mythology)
96	**perverse** difficult
97	**but else ... world** but otherwise, I wouldn't behave in such a way for anything in the world
98	**fond** foolishly (head over heels) in love
99	**haviour light** behaviour 'forward'
101	**those ... strange** girls who have more skill to play hard to get
103	**But that** if it were not for the fact that
105	**not ... love** do not put my willingness to love you down to frivolous love
106	**discovered** revealed
110	**That ... orb** that changes her orbit every month
114	**god of my idolatry** the god that I worship (idolise)
117	**contract** exchange of statements of love
118	**unadvised** badly thought out
121–2	**This bud ... meet** Juliet compares their love which is so new to a flower bud which in warm summer weather will quickly open out into a full flower. Their love will do this by the next time they meet.
125–6	**O wilt ... tonight?** Romeo does not want to leave, but Juliet apparently misunderstands what he means by 'unsatisfied'.

They say Jove laughs. O gentle Romeo,
If thou dost love, pronounce it faithfully.
Or if thou thinkest I am too quickly won,   95
I'll frown and be perverse, and say thee nay,
So thou wilt woo; but else not for the world.
In truth fair Montague I am too fond,
And therefore thou mayst think my haviour light.
But trust me gentleman, I'll prove more true   100
Than those that have more cunning to be strange.
I should have been more strange, I must confess,
But that thou overheard'st, ere I was ware,
My true-love passion. Therefore pardon me,
And not impute this yielding to light love,   105
Which the dark night hath so discovered.

ROMEO   Lady, by yonder blessed moon I vow,
That tips with silver all these fruit-tree tops –

JULIET   O swear not by the moon, th' inconstant moon,
That monthly changes in her circled orb,   110
Lest that thy love prove likewise variable.

ROMEO   What shall I swear by?

JULIET   Do not swear at all;
Or if thou wilt, swear by thy gracious self,
Which is the god of my idolatry,
And I'll believe thee.

ROMEO   If my heart's dear love –   115

JULIET   Well do not swear. Although I joy in thee,
I have no joy of this contract tonight.
It is too rash, too unadvised, too sudden;
Too like the lightning, which doth cease to be
Ere one can say, 'It lightens'. Sweet, good night.   120
This bud of love by summer's ripening breath
May prove a beauteous flower when next we meet.
Good night, good night. As sweet response and rest
Come to thy heart, as that within my breast.

ROMEO   O wilt thou leave me so unsatisfied?   125

JULIET   What satisfaction canst thou have tonight?

Romeo begs her at least to exchange vows of love with him. The Nurse calls Juliet away. When Juliet returns she says that she will send a messenger to Romeo that day to arrange a time and place where they can be married. Then she goes into the house.

129	**I would** I wish
131	**frank** generous
133	**bounty** generosity
	boundless without limits
141	**Too ... substantial** too good to be true
143	**bent of love** intentions
145	**procure** arrange
146	**rite** ceremony
150	**anon** straight away
151	**beseech** beg
152	**cease thy strife** stop trying so hard
153	**send** send someone with a message

ROMEO	Th' exchange of thy love's faithful vow for mine.
JULIET	I gave thee mine before thou didst request it;
	And yet I would it were to give again. 129
ROMEO	Wouldst thou withdraw it? For what purpose, love?
JULIET	But to be frank and give it thee again.
	And yet I wish but for the thing I have.
	My bounty is as boundless as the sea,
	My love as deep; the more I give to thee
	The more I have, for both are infinite. 135
	I hear some noise within; dear love adieu.

[NURSE *calls within*

Anon good Nurse! Sweet Montague, be true.
Stay but a little, I will come again. [*Exit*

ROMEO	O blessed, blessed night! I am afeard,
	Being in night, all this is but a dream, 140
	Too flattering-sweet to be substantial.

Enter JULIET *again*

JULIET	Three words, dear Romeo, and good night indeed.
	If that thy bent of love be honourable,
	Thy purpose marriage, send me word tomorrow,
	By one that I'll procure to come to thee, 145
	Where and what time thou wilt perform the rite;
	And all my fortunes at thy foot I'll lay,
	And follow thee my lord throughout the world.
NURSE	[*Within*] Madam!
JULIET	I come, anon – But if thou mean'st not well, 150
	I do beseech thee –
NURSE	[*Within*] Madam!
JULIET	By and by, I come –
	To cease thy strife, and leave me to my grief.
	Tomorrow will I send.
ROMEO	So thrive my soul –
JULIET	A thousand times good night. [*Exit*
ROMEO	A thousand times the worse, to want thy light. 155

A moment later Juliet returns; she has forgotten to fix a time at which Romeo will meet her messenger.

156–7   **Love goes … looks** In other words two lovers go towards each other as fast as the schoolboy goes away from school, and vice versa.

159   **tassel-gentle** male falcon (They were highly prized by falconers. If one went off on its own, the falconer had to use a special call to bring it back again.)

160   **Bondage … aloud** Juliet is 'tied up' (in bondage) because she is not supposed to be speaking to a young man in this way so she has to use a loud whisper (hoarse) rather than calling him.

161   **Echo** In mythology a nymph who was in love with Narcissus. She could not speak her love for him, but was condemned to repeat the end of whatever people said to her.

166   **attending** listening

167   **nyas** a young hawk that cannot yet fly

177   **wanton** naughty child

179   **gyves** chains

182   **I would I were** I wish I was

Love goes toward love as schoolboys from their
    books,
But love from love, toward school with heavy looks.

Enter JULIET *again*

JULIET
Hist, Romeo, hist! O for a falconer's voice,
To lure this tassel-gentle back again.
Bondage is hoarse, and may not speak aloud,   160
Else would I tear the cave where Echo lies,
And make her airy tongue more hoarse than mine
With repetition of my 'Romeo'

ROMEO
It is my soul that calls upon my name.
How silver-sweet sound lovers' tongues by night,   165
Like softest music to attending ears.

JULIET
Romeo!

ROMEO
        My nyas?

JULIET
                What o'clock tomorrow
Shall I send to thee?

ROMEO
                    By the hour of nine.

JULIET
I will not fail; 'tis twenty years till then.
I have forgot why I did call thee back.   170

ROMEO
Let me stand here till thou remember it.

JULIET
I shall forget, to have thee still stand there,
Remembering how I love thy company.

ROMEO
And I'll still stay, to have thee still forget,
Forgetting any other home but this.   175

JULIET
'Tis almost morning; I would have thee gone,
And yet no farther than a wanton's bird,
Who lets it hop a little from her hand,
Like a poor prisoner in his twisted gyves,
And with a silken thread plucks it back again,   180
So loving-jealous of his liberty.

ROMEO
I would I were thy bird.

JULIET
                    Sweet, so would I.
Yet I should kill thee with much cherishing.

93

At last they part. Juliet goes back into the house and Romeo leaves the garden and goes on his way.

187   **Would ... rest** Romeo wishes that he was 'sleep' and 'peace' so that he could stay close to Juliet.

189   **crave** beg

my dear hap the wonderful thing that has happened to me

Act 2 scenes 1 and 2

Staging solutions

When we read Act 2 scenes 1 and 2 it is important to get a clear picture of:

- what is going on
- how it would have been staged in Shakespeare's theatre.

Work on your own

1   Think about the answers to these questions.

   a   Where does scene 1 take place?

   b   Where does Romeo go after line 2?

   c   Where is Romeo for the rest of the scene? (Before you answer this question, look at Romeo's first line in scene 2. What does this tell us about where he was during the rest of scene 1?)

   d   Where is Romeo at the beginning of scene 2?

Work with a partner

2   Discuss your answers to the questions above.

Good night, good night. Parting is such sweet
   sorrow,
That I shall say 'Good night' till it be morrow.   185

                                       [*Exit*

ROMEO   Sleep dwell upon thine eyes, peace in thy breast.
           Would I were sleep and peace, so sweet to rest.
           Hence will I to my ghostly father's cell,
           His help to crave, and my dear hap to tell.

                                       [*Exit*

ACTIVITIES

3 Now look at the pictures of Shakespeare's theatre on pages 8–11
and think about how scene 1 and the beginning of scene 2 could
have been staged. Use the plan of the stage below to help you.

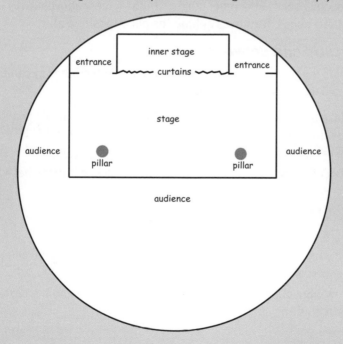

One solution

One way of staging the beginning of scene 1 could have been like this:

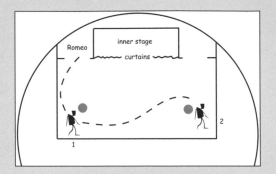

- Romeo enters from the back.
- He comes down to the front corner of the stage to speak his two lines (position 1).
- He looks back at the inner stage with the gallery above it. This is Juliet's house. He moves behind the pillar (position 2).

Mercutio and Benvolio

Now it is the turn of Mercutio and Benvolio to enter, but they can't see Romeo because he is 'hidden' by the pillar.

4 Make a copy of the stage diagram, just marking Romeo's final position (2).

5 Read the scene again and think about where Benvolio and Mercutio might move. Remember that this scene is funny because:

   a Romeo can hear Mercutio making fun of him.
     (How does he feel?)

   b We know this, but Mercutio and Benvolio don't.

6 On your stage plan, mark the moves of Mercutio and Benvolio until the end of the scene.

7 Now work out how Romeo moves from this scene into the next. Mark this on your plan.

Quotation quiz

For each of these quotations, work out:

1 who said it
2 who they were speaking to
3 where they are
4 what the action is.

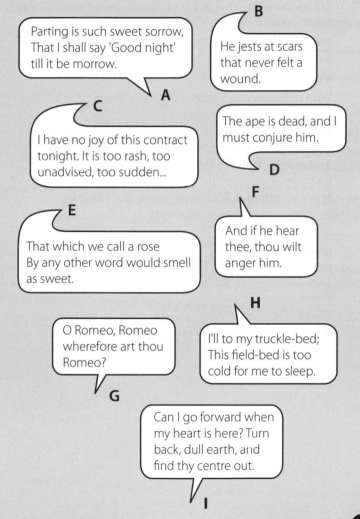

A
Parting is such sweet sorrow,
That I shall say 'Good night'
till it be morrow.

B
He jests at scars
that never felt a
wound.

C
I have no joy of this contract
tonight. It is too rash, too
unadvised, too sudden...

D
The ape is dead, and I
must conjure him.

E
That which we call a rose
By any other word would smell
as sweet.

F
And if he hear
thee, thou wilt
anger him.

G
O Romeo, Romeo
wherefore art thou
Romeo?

H
I'll to my truckle-bed;
This field-bed is too
cold for me to sleep.

I
Can I go forward when
my heart is here? Turn
back, dull earth, and
find thy centre out.

Romeo visits his confessor and spiritual adviser, Friar Lawrence. He finds the Friar collecting herbs.

1   **grey-eyed morn** as the light grows the night is no longer so black

2   **Chequering** patterning

3   **fleckled darkness** a mixture of 'flecked' and 'dappled': there are spots and patches of light on the darkness.

4   **From forth** away from

     Titan's burning wheels the wheels of the sun-god's chariot which brings daylight to the world

5   **ere** before

     advance lift

7   **osier cage** wicker basket

8   **With ... flowers** with herbs that can deliver poison and flowers that can heal

9–10 **The earth ... womb** The earth is both a tomb, where all life goes when it dies, and a womb from which all new life comes

11–12 **And from ... find** we humans use all sorts of plants that the earth produces

13–14 **Many ... different** many with several good health-giving properties; all offering some variety

15   **mickle** great

     grace healing qualities

17–20 **For nought ... abuse** There is nothing living that does not have some special value and nothing is so good that it cannot go wrong if abused

21–2 **Virtue ... dignified** Virtue wrongly used can become vice and even vice in its effects can produce good

Scene ❸

Outside Friar Lawrence's cell
Enter FRIAR LAWRENCE *with a basket*

F. LAWRENCE   The grey-eyed morn smiles on the frowning night,
Chequering the eastern clouds with streaks of light;
And fleckled darkness like a drunkard reels
From forth day's path and Titan's burning wheels.
Now ere the sun advance his burning eye,   5
The day to cheer, and night's dank dew to dry,
I must up-fill this osier cage of ours
With baleful weeds, and precious-juiced flowers.
The earth that's nature's mother is her tomb;
What is her burying grave, that is her womb;   10
And from her womb children of divers kind
We sucking on her natural bosom find;
Many for many virtues excellent,
None but for some, and yet all different.
O mickle is the powerful grace that lies   15
In plants, herbs, stones, and their true qualities.
For nought so vile that on the earth doth live,
But to the earth some special good doth give,
Nor aught so good, but strained from that fair use,
Revolts from true birth, stumbling on abuse.   20
Virtue itself turns vice being misapplied,
And vice sometime's by action dignified.

Enter ROMEO

It is very early in the morning and Friar Lawrence deduces correctly that Romeo has been out all night. Romeo admits this.

23–6   **Within ... heart** the skin of this plant contains both poison and medicine, if you smell it; it does you good; if you swallow it, you die

27–8   **Two ... will** In humans too there are the same opposites, great good and evil

29–30   **And where ... plant** where the evil intention is stronger, death soon follows

31   **Benedicite** (Latin) God bless you

33–4   **it argues ... bed** being up so early suggests that you are worried about something

35–6   **Care ... lie** Old men have plenty to worry about and if you are worried you don't sleep well

37   **unstuffed** unworried

40   **up-roused ... distemperature** awoken by some worry

45   **ghostly** spiritual

50–1   **one hath wounded ... wounded** someone wounded me (with love) and I wounded them in the same way

52   **physic** medicine

54   **My intercession ... foe** the request I am making to you will also help my 'enemy'

55   **thy drift** what you are saying

56   **Riddling ... shrift** if you confess to me using words I can't understand, you will only get a forgiveness that you can't understand

Within the infant rind of this weak flower
Poison hath residence, and medicine power;
For this being smelt with that part cheers each part; 25
Being tasted, stays all senses with the heart.
Two such opposed kings encamp them still
In man as well as herbs – grace and rude will;
And where the worser is predominant,
Full soon the canker death eats up that plant. 30

ROMEO Good morrow father.

F. LAWRENCE *Benedicite*!
What early tongue so sweet saluteth me?
Young son, it argues a distempered head
So soon to bid good morrow to thy bed.
Care keeps his watch in every old man's eye, 35
And where care lodges, sleep will never lie;
But where unbruised youth with unstuffed brain
Doth couch his limbs, there golden sleep doth reign.
Therefore thy earliness doth me assure
Thou art up-roused with some distemperature; 40
Or if not so, then here I hit it right,
Our Romeo hath not been in bed tonight.

ROMEO That last is true; the sweeter rest was mine.

F. LAWRENCE God pardon sin, wast thou with Rosaline?

ROMEO With Rosaline, my ghostly father? No. 45
I have forgot that name, and that name's woe.

F. LAWRENCE That's my good son; but where hast thou been
then?

ROMEO I'll tell thee ere thou ask it me again.
I have been feasting with mine enemy,
Where on a sudden one hath wounded me, 50
That's by me wounded; both our remedies
Within thy help and holy physic lies.
I bear no hatred, blessed man; for lo,
My intercession likewise steads my foe.

F. LAWRENCE Be plain good son, and homely in thy drift; 55
Riddling confession finds but riddling shrift.

Romeo tells Friar Lawrence that he has fallen in love with Juliet, a Capulet. Friar Lawrence points out that only yesterday he was just as deeply in love with Rosaline. He points out that Romeo's love for Rosaline was not true love.

59–61 **As mine ... marriage** She is as much in love with me as I am in love with her. So our loves are perfectly joined, except for what you have to do, which is marry us

63 **pass** go along

65 **Saint Francis** the founder of the religious order to which Friar Lawrence belongs

69 **brine** salt water

70 **sallow** pale

77–8 **If e'er ... Rosaline** If you were being yourself and talking about real unhappiness, then both you and your unhappiness were all about Rosaline

79 **sentence** proverb

80 **Women ... men** When men are weak then what hope is there for women?

81 **chidst me** told me off

82 **For doting ... loving** for being infatuated (imagining you were in love) not for truly loving

83 **bad'st me** told me

85–6 **her I ... allow** the person I love now gives me favours in return for the favours I give her; she shares her love with me as I share mine with her

88 **Thy ... spell** your love was like someone who 'reads' by learning the story by heart but cannot spell out the letters of what is written

ROMEO	Then plainly know my heart's dear love is set	
	On the fair daughter of rich Capulet.	
	As mine on hers, so hers is set on mine,	
	And all combined, save what thou must combine	60
	By holy marriage. When, and where, and how,	
	We met, we wooed, and made exchange of vow,	
	I'll tell thee as we pass; but this I pray,	
	That thou consent to marry us today.	
F. LAWRENCE	Holy Saint Francis, what a change is here!	65
	Is Rosaline, whom thou didst love so dear,	
	So soon forsaken? Young men's love then lies	
	Not truly in their hearts, but in their eyes.	
	Jesu Maria, what a deal of brine	
	Hath washed thy sallow cheeks for Rosaline!	70
	How much salt water thrown away in waste,	
	To season love, that of it doth not taste!	
	The sun not yet thy sighs from heaven clears,	
	Thy old groans ring yet in mine ancient ears;	
	Lo here upon thy cheek the stain doth sit	75
	Of an old tear that is not washed off yet.	
	If e'er thou wast thyself, and these woes thine,	
	Thou and these woes were all for Rosaline.	
	And art thou changed? Pronounce this sentence then,	
	Women may fall, when there's no strength in men.	80
ROMEO	Thou chid'st me oft for loving Rosaline.	
F. LAWRENCE	For doting, not for loving, pupil mine.	
ROMEO	And bad'st me bury love.	
F. LAWRENCE	Not in a grave,	
	To lay one in another out to have.	
ROMEO	I pray thee chide me not; her I love now	85
	Doth grace for grace, and love for love allow.	
	The other did not so.	
F. LAWRENCE	O she knew well	
	Thy love did read by rote, that could not spell.	

Friar Lawrence accepts that Romeo's love for Juliet may be true love and that the relationship between them may serve to bring their warring families together.

89	**waverer** person who keeps on changing his/her mind
91	**alliance** marriage (but also an alliance between the two families)
92	**rancour** hatred

Later that morning Mercutio and Benvolio are still looking for Romeo. Tybalt has sent a letter (probably a challenge) to Romeo's home.

4   **wench** woman

5   **run mad** go mad

12–15   **he is ... butt-shaft** Mercutio claims that Romeo is as good as dead as he has been so weakened by being in love.

15   **blind bow-boy** Cupid, the god of love

         butt-shaft an arrow made for shooting at a target

16   **encounter** fight

18   **Cats** Tybalt's name reminds Mercutio of the name of a cat in an old fable.

But come young waverer, come go with me.
In one respect I'll thy assistant be;   90
For this alliance may so happy prove,
To turn your households' rancour to pure love.

ROMEO   O let us hence, I stand on sudden haste.

F. LAWRENCE   Wisely and slow, they stumble that run fast.

[Exeunt

Scene ❹

A street in Verona
Enter BENVOLIO *and* MERCUTIO

MERCUTIO   Where the devil should this Romeo be?
               Came he not home tonight?

BENVOLIO   Not to his father's; I spoke with his man.

MERCUTIO   Why, that same pale hard-hearted wench, that
                   Rosaline,
               Torments him so, that he will sure run mad.   5

BENVOLIO   Tybalt, the kinsman to old Capulet,
               Hath sent a letter to his father's house.

MERCUTIO   A challenge, on my life.

BENVOLIO   Romeo will answer it.

MERCUTIO   Any man that can write may answer a letter.

BENVOLIO   Nay, he will answer the letter's master, how he   10
               dares, being dared.

MERCUTIO   Alas poor Romeo, he is already dead, stabbed with
               a white wench's black eye, run through the
               ear with a lovesong, the very pin of his heart cleft
               with the blind bow-boy's butt-shaft; and is he a   15
               man to encounter Tybalt?

BENVOLIO   Why what is Tybalt?

MERCUTIO   More than Prince of Cats. O he is the

Mercutio comments that Tybalt loves duelling and knows all the latest fencing styles. Romeo arrives and greets them.

19   **captain of compliments** master of polite ceremonies

20–1   **prick-song ... proportion** Tybalt's fencing is compared with singing from printed music. His duelling is accurately paced.

22–3   **butcher ... button** a duellist who demonstrates his skill by flicking off a button from his opponent's doublet

23–4   **a gentleman ... house** a graduate of the finest school of fencing

25–6   *passado* **... hay!** Continental terms for fencing thrusts. Benvolio makes it clear they are foreign as he is not familiar with them.

28–9   **The pox ... accents** A curse on these affected people and their phoney accents

29–31   **'By Jesu ... whore!'** phrases the friends are more used to

32   **grandsire** pretending Benvolio is an old man who regrets new manners

33–4   **flies ... 'pardon-me's'** foreigners using the latest words in fashion

38   **Without his roe** Both because Romeo is sighing 'me, O' and so lacking the first syllable of his name and because 'roe' is the sexually active part of the fish.

40   **Petrarch** A famous poet. Mercutio goes on to claim that none of the famous lovers of history can compare with Romeo's Rosaline. He doesn't know about the change in Romeo's affections.

41–4   **Laura ... Thisbe** Petrarch was in love with Laura. The other characters mentioned come from Greek and Roman stories.

43–4   **hildings and harlots** loose women

46   **French slop** baggy breeches: Romeo is still wearing the clothes he wore to the Capulets' party.

47   **the counterfeit** the slip

53   **courtesy** politeness

courageous captain of compliments. He fights as
you sing prick-song, keeps time, distance, and   20
proportion; rests me his minim rests, one, two, and
the third in your bosom; the very butcher of a
silk button, a duellist, a duellist; a gentleman of
the very first house, of the first and second cause.
Ah the immortal *passado*, the *punto reverso*, the   25
hay!

BENVOLIO   The what?

MERCUTIO   The pox of such antic lisping affecting
phantacimes, these new tuners of accents! 'By
Jesu a very good blade – a very tall man – a very   30
good whore!' Why, is not this a lamentable
thing, grandsire, that we should be thus afflicted
with these strange flies, these fashion-mongers,
these 'pardon-me's', who stand so much on the
new form that they cannot sit at ease on the old   35
bench? O their bones, their bones!

Enter ROMEO.

BENVOLIO   Here comes Romeo, here comes Romeo.

MERCUTIO   Without his roe, like a dried herring. O flesh,
flesh, how art thou fishified! Now is he for the
numbers that Petrarch flowed in. Laura to his   40
lady was a kitchen-wench – marry, she had a
better love to be-rhyme her – Dido a dowdy,
Cleopatra a gipsy, Helen and Hero hildings and
harlots, Thisbe a grey eye or so, but not to the
purpose – Signor Romeo, *bon jour*. There's a   45
French salutation to your French slop. You gave
us the counterfeit fairly last night.

ROMEO   Good morrow to you both. What counterfeit did
I give you?

MERCUTIO   The slip sir, the slip, can you not conceive?   50

ROMEO   Pardon good Mercutio, my business was great,
and in such a case as mine a man may strain
courtesy.

Romeo is in fine form and is more than a match for Mercutio's skill with words.

55   **constrains** forces

bow in the hams bend from the waist

56   **curtsy** Romeo plays on the word 'courtesy'.

59   **pink** 1) height 2) a garden flower

62   **pump** a light shoe for dancing

63–6   **Sure ... singular** The witty exchanges continue with **puns** on 'shoe sole', 'soul' and 'solely'.

67   **single-soled** thin

69   **Come between us** Keep us apart

70–1   **Switch and spurs** Keep it going: a horse would be encouraged to go faster with whip (switch) and spurs.

72   **wild-goose chase** A kind of horse-race where follow-my-leader was played until the lead changed over.

73–81 **for thou ... sauce** A battle of wits between the two men with quick puns on 'goose': 1) goose is supposed to be stupid so 2) a fool, until we reach the idea of 3) goose as dinner

80   **sweeting** a sweet apple variety

84   **cheverel** a flexible kid-leather

84–5   **an inch narrow** Romeo's small wit

ell a measure of length, 112 cm (45 inches)

86   **broad** 1) obvious 2) large 3) indecent

MERCUTIO	That's as much as to say, such a case as yours constrains a man to bow in the hams.	
ROMEO	Meaning to curtsy.	55
MERCUTIO	Thou hast most kindly hit it.	
ROMEO	A most courteous exposition.	
MERCUTIO	Nay I am the very pink of courtesy.	
ROMEO	Pink for flower.	60
MERCUTIO	Right.	
ROMEO	Why then is my pump well flowered.	
MERCUTIO	Sure wit. Follow me this jest now, till thou hast worn out thy pump, that when the single sole of it is worn, the jest may remain after the wearing solely singular.	65
ROMEO	O single-soled jest, solely singular for the singleness.	
MERCUTIO	Come between us good Benvolio, my wits faint.	
ROMEO	Switch and spurs, switch and spurs, or I'll cry a match.	70
MERCUTIO	Nay, if our wits run the wild-goose chase, I am done; for thou hast more of the wild-goose in one of thy wits than I am sure I have in my whole five. Was I with you there for the goose?	75
ROMEO	Thou wast never with me for anything when thou wast not there for the goose.	
MERCUTIO	I will bite thee by the ear for that jest.	
ROMEO	Nay good goose, bite not.	
MERCUTIO	Thy wit is a very bitter sweeting, it is a most sharp sauce.	80
ROMEO	And is it not well served in to a sweet goose?	
MERCUTIO	O here's a wit of cheverel that stretches from an inch narrow to an ell broad.	85
ROMEO	I stretch it out for that word 'broad', which,	

When the Nurse and her attendant Peter come looking for Romeo, the three young men tease her mercilessly.

91–2   **Now art ... by nature** Now you are yourself – both in your nature and also in the skills you have learned in conversation and wit

92   **drivelling** 1) slobbering 2) talking nonsense

93   **natural** half-wit

94   **bauble** 1) worthless trinket 2) stick carried by the court fool 3) penis

96–101 **Thou desirest ... longer** A series of bawdy **puns** triggered by the word 'bauble' and playing on words: 'tale' (story)/'tail' (penis).

102   **Goodly gear** The nurse comes sailing along, her clothes billowing out.

109   **God ye** God give you

112–13 **the bawdy ... noon** Mercutio tells her the time in a deliberately obscene way.

116   **mar** spoil

118   **quoth a!** he says, does he?!

	added to the goose proves thee far and wide a broad goose.	
MERCUTIO	Why, is not this better now than groaning for love? Now art thou sociable, now art thou Romeo. Now art thou what thou art, by art as well as by nature, for this drivelling love is like a great natural that runs lolling up and down to hide his bauble in a hole.	90
BENVOLIO	Stop there, stop there.	95
MERCUTIO	Thou desirest me to stop in my tale against the hair.	
BENVOLIO	Thou wouldst else have made thy tale large.	
MERCUTIO	O thou art deceived; I would have made it short, for I was come to the whole depth of my tale, and meant indeed to occupy the argument no longer.	100

Enter NURSE *and* PETER

ROMEO	Here's goodly gear! A sail, a sail!	
MERCUTIO	Two, two; a shirt and a smock.	
NURSE	Peter.	
PETER	Anon.	105
NURSE	My fan Peter.	
MERCUTIO	Good Peter, to hide her face, for her fan's the fairer face.	
NURSE	God ye good morrow gentlemen.	
MERCUTIO	God ye good den fair gentlewoman.	110
NURSE	Is it good den?	
MERCUTIO	'Tis no less, I tell ye, for the bawdy hand of the dial is now upon the prick of noon.	
NURSE	Out upon you, what a man are you!	
ROMEO	One, gentlewoman, that God hath made for himself to mar.	115
NURSE	By my troth, it is well said 'for himself to mar', quoth a! Gentlemen, can any of you tell me	

At last Mercutio and Benvolio leave and the Nurse can speak to Romeo.

122 **when you sought him** when you started looking for him

123 **for ... worse** for lack of a worse person

127 **confidence** private conversation

128 **indite** invite

129 **a bawd** a person who keeps a brothel (Mercutio is suggesting that the Nurse wants to make an improper suggestion to Romeo.)

So ho! a hunting call used when the game has been sighted

131 **lenten pie** During Lent no meat was eaten, so a hare pie would be stale, having been made before Lent.

133 **hoar** grey with age (but a **play on words** with 'whore' (prostitute) and 'hare')

137 **too ... score** not worth putting on the list of game you have caught

138 **spent** used up (and sexually exhausted)

145 **ropery** trickery

148 **stand to** put up with

149 **'a** he

150 **lustier** stronger

151 **Jacks** villains

152 **Scurvy knave** Wicked villain

flirt-gills women of loose morals

	where I may find the young Romeo?
ROMEO	I can tell you, but young Romeo will be older 120
	when you have found him, than he was when
	you sought him. I am the youngest of that name,
	for fault of a worse.
NURSE	You say well.
MERCUTIO	Yea, is the worst well? Very well took, i' faith, 125
	wisely, wisely.
NURSE	If you be he sir, I desire some confidence with you.
BENVOLIO	She will indite him to some supper.
MERCUTIO	A bawd, a bawd, a bawd! So ho!
ROMEO	What hast thou found? 130
MERCUTIO	No hare sir, unless a hare sir in a lenten pie, that
	is something stale and hoar ere it be spent.

MERCUTIO
    [*Sings*] An old hare hoar,
        And an old hare hoar,
        Is very good meat in Lent: 135
        But a hare that is hoar
        Is too much for a score,
        When it hoars ere it be spent.

MERCUTIO	Romeo, will you come to your father's? We'll to
	dinner thither. 140
ROMEO	I will follow you.
MERCUTIO	Farewell ancient lady, farewell,
	[*Sings*] lady, lady, lady.
	[*Exeunt* MERCUTIO *and* BENVOLIO
NURSE	I pray you sir, what saucy merchant was this that
	was so full of his ropery? 145
ROMEO	A gentleman, Nurse, that loves to hear himself
	talk, and will speak more in a minute than he will
	stand to in a month.
NURSE	And 'a speak to anything against me, I'll take him
	down, an 'a were lustier than he is, and twenty 150
	such Jacks; and if I cannot, I'll find those that
	shall. Scurvy knave, I am none of his flirt-gills, I

The Nurse gives Romeo her message, but not before expressing her indignation at the way she has been treated and giving Romeo a warning about treating Juliet properly. Then she arranges with Romeo that Juliet will go to Friar Lawrence's cell that afternoon to be married.

153 **skain's-mates** women of loose morals

154 **suffer** allow

155 **use ... pleasure** take advantage of me (She means 'make fun' of her, but it has an accidental bawdy double meaning, which she doesn't realise.)

156–7 **I saw ... out** Peter repeats the double meaning (not realising it) and his comment about his 'weapon' only makes it worse.

162 **Scurvy knave!** Dirty beast!

163–4 **bade ... out** told me to find you by asking around

166 **lead ... paradise** seduce her by pretending to offer marriage

167 **gross** wicked

169 **deal double with** cheat

171 **weak dealing** bad behaviour (The Nurse means to say something much stronger, but not for the first time she comes out with the wrong words.)

172 **commend me to** give my greetings to

176–7 **dost not mark** are not listening to

181 **shrift** confession

183 **shrived and married** Before marriage the couple confessed their sins and were given absolution (forgiveness).

	am none of his skain's-mates! [*To* PETER] And	
	thou must stand by too, and suffer every knave	
	to use me at his pleasure?	155
PETER	I saw no man use you at his pleasure. If I had,	
	my weapon should quickly have been out, I	
	warrant you; I dare draw as soon as another	
	man, if I see occasion in a good quarrel, and the	
	law on my side.	160
NURSE	Now afore God I am so vexed, that every part	
	about me quivers. Scurvy knave! Pray you sir a	
	word and as I told you, my young lady bade me	
	inquire you out. What she bade me say, I will	
	keep to myself. But first let me tell ye, if ye	165
	should lead her in a fool's paradise, as they say, it	
	were a very gross kind of behaviour, as they say;	
	for the gentlewoman is young, and therefore if	
	you should deal double with her, truly it were an	
	ill thing to be offered to any gentlewoman, and	170
	very weak dealing.	
ROMEO	Nurse, commend me to thy lady and mistress. I,	
	protest unto thee –	
NURSE	Good heart, and i' faith, I will tell her as much.	
	Lord, Lord, she will be a joyful woman.	175
ROMEO	What wilt thou tell her, Nurse? Thou dost not	
	mark me.	
NURSE	I will tell her sir, that you do protest, which as I	
	take it is a gentlemanlike offer.	
ROMEO	Bid her devise	180
	Some means to come to shrift this afternoon,	
	And there she shall at Friar Lawrence's cell	
	Be shrived and married. Here is for thy pains.	
NURSE	No truly sir, not a penny.	
ROMEO	Go to, I say you shall.	185
NURSE	This afternoon sir? Well, she shall be there.	
romeo	And stay good Nurse behind the abbey wall,	

They also arrange that a rope ladder will be hidden at the Capulets' house for Romeo to get in that night.

189	**cords ... stair** a rope ladder	
190–1	**which ... night** which must carry me under cover of darkness to the summit of my happiness	
190	**high top-gallant** top of the tallest mast (of a sailing ship)	
192	**quit thy pains** pay you for your trouble	
197	**Two ... away** two people can keep a secret, but three can't (a **proverb**)	
198	**warrant thee** I promise you	
200	**prating** chattering	
201–2	**would ... aboard** has designs on her	
202	**had as lief** would as soon	
204	**properer** better-looking	
206	**clout** rag, piece of cloth	
	the versal world the whole world	
207	**rosemary** a herb that was said to stand for remembrance	
210	**that's the dog's name** (because if you say 'R' it sounds like a dog growling)	
210–11	**R ... no** The Nurse is someone who starts to speak before she has worked out what she is going to say. She was probably going to say 'arse' – in which case she's no good at spelling, either.	
212	**sententious** She means 'sentence', i.e. a saying.	

Within this hour my man shall be with thee,
And bring thee cords made like a tackled stair,
Which to the high top-gallant of my joy   190
Must be my convoy in the secret night.
Farewell, be trusty, and I'll quit thy pains.
Farewell, commend me to thy mistress.

NURSE   Now God in heaven bless thee. Hark you sir,

ROMEO   What sayest thou my dear Nurse?   195

NURSE   Is your man secret? Did you ne'er hear say,
Two may keep counsel, putting one away?

ROMEO   I warrant thee my man's as true as steel.

NURSE   Well sir, my mistress is the sweetest lady. Lord,
Lord, when 't was a little prating thing. O there   200
is a nobleman in town, one Paris, that would fain
lay knife aboard; but she good soul had as lief see
a toad, a very toad, as see him. I anger her
sometimes, and tell her that Paris is the properer
man; but I'll warrant you when I say so, she   205
looks as pale as any clout in the versal world.
Doth not rosemary and Romeo begin with
a letter?

ROMEO   Ay Nurse, what of that? Both with an R?

NURSE   Ah mocker, that's the dog-name; R is for the –   210
no, I know it begins with some other letter. And
she hath the prettiest sententious of it, of you
and rosemary, that it would do you good to hear
it.

ROMEO   Commend me to thy lady.

NURSE   Ay, a thousand times. Peter!   215

PETER   Anon.

NURSE   Before and apace.

[*Exeunt*

Act 2 scenes 3 and 4

Character: Friar Lawrence

This is the first time we have met the Friar, who will come to play an important part in the lives of Romeo and Juliet. He was Romeo's confessor, the priest to whom he confessed his sins and from whom he received forgiveness. It is obvious that he knows Romeo very well. Act 2 scene 3 gives us a good picture of the Friar and of his relationship with Romeo.

Work on your own

1   Make a list of at least five words that describe the Friar's character. You can choose from the list below, or think of your own words.

Warning: The list contains a number of words that do not describe the Friar well.

irritable	fatherly	strict	lonely
forgetful	intelligent	jokey	God-fearing
knowledgeable	forgiving	nervous	thoughtful
solitary	paternalistic	observant	impatient

2   For each of the words you have chosen, find some **evidence** to support your choice. Copy the table below and use it to record your ideas.

3   Use the 'Explanation' column to link the word you have chosen and the evidence you have found.

Point	Evidence	Explanation
knowledgeable	lines 15–16	He knows all the 'true qualities' of the herbs he is collecting.

Character: Mercutio

Moods

Mercutio's moods change suddenly and frequently and it must be difficult for other characters to know how to 'take him'.

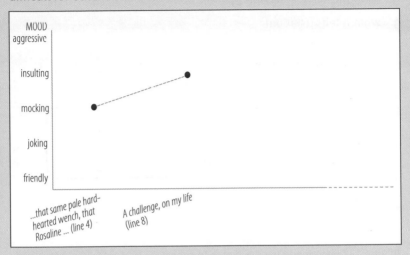

Work with a partner

1 On a large sheet of paper, draw the 'mood temperature' graph shown above and then plot in pencil how and why Mercutio's mood changes during Act 2 scene 4. The graph has been started to show you how to do the task.

Join with another pair

2 Compare your graphs. Discuss the differences. Change and/or add to your graph if you wish.

Qualities

Work on your own

Now make a Point/Evidence/Explanation table for Mercutio. Here are some adjectives to choose from:

clever	comatose	sensitive	lonely
show-off	selfish	morose	sociable
bawdy	witty	quick-witted	handsome

Quotation quiz

For each of these quotations, work out:

1   who said it
2   who they were speaking to
3   what it tells us about
    a   the speaker
    b   any other characters.

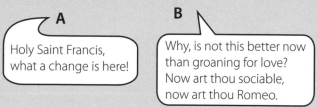

> **A**
> Holy Saint Francis, what a change is here!

> **B**
> Why, is not this better now than groaning for love? Now art thou sociable, now art thou Romeo.

Juliet waits impatiently for the Nurse to return.

3   **Perchance** Perhaps
5   **Which ... beams** which travel ten times faster than the speed of light
6   **lowering** overhanging, threatening
7   **nimble-pinioned** swift-winged
        draw love In classical pictures doves were shown drawing a chariot containing Venus, the goddess of love.
8   **wind-swift** as fast as the wind
9–10   **Now ... journey** it is midday

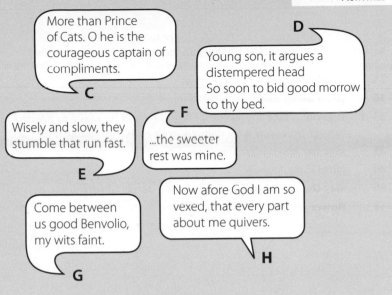

C
More than Prince of Cats. O he is the courageous captain of compliments.

D
Young son, it argues a distempered head So soon to bid good morrow to thy bed.

E
Wisely and slow, they stumble that run fast.

F
...the sweeter rest was mine.

G
Come between us good Benvolio, my wits faint.

H
Now afore God I am so vexed, that every part about me quivers.

Scene 5

Capulet's mansion
Enter JULIET

JULIET   The clock struck nine when I did send the Nurse;
In half an hour she promised to return.
Perchance she cannot meet him – that's not so –
O she is lame, love's heralds should be thoughts,
Which ten times faster glides than the sun's beams, 5
Driving back shadows over lowering hills.
Therefore do nimble-pinioned doves draw love,
And therefore hath the wind-swift Cupid wings
Now is the sun upon the highmost hill
Of this day's journey, and from nine to twelve 10
Is three long hours, yet she is not come.
Had she affections and warm youthful blood,

When the Nurse returns, she is in no hurry to tell Juliet what has happened. She teases Juliet by delaying her news as long as possible.

14   **bandy** send back (as in tennis)

16   **feign as** act as if

23–4   **If good ... face** If your news is good it will be music to my ears but you will spoil it by telling it with such a miserable face

25   **give me leave** leave me alone

26   **jaunt** tiring journey

36   **stay the circumstance** wait for the details of your message

44   **flower** model

She would be as swift in motion as a ball;
My words would bandy her to my sweet love,
And his to me.   15
But old folks, many feign as they were dead,
Unwieldy, slow, heavy and pale as lead.
O God she comes! O honey Nurse what news?

Enter NURSE *and* PETER

Hast thou met with him? Send thy man away.

NURSE   Peter, stay at the gate.   [*Exit* PETER 20

JULIET   Now good sweet Nurse – O Lord why lookest
              thou sad?
         Though news be sad, yet tell them merrily.
         If good, thou sham'st the music of sweet news
         By playing it to me with so sour a face.

NURSE   I am aweary, give me leave awhile.   25
         Fie how my bones ache, what a jaunt have I!

JULIET   I would thou hadst my bones, and I thy news.
         Nay come I pray thee speak, good, good Nurse,
              speak.

NURSE   Jesu, what haste! Can you not stay awhile?
         Do you not see that I am out of breath?   30

JULIET   How art thou out of breath, when thou hast breath
         To say to me that thou art out of breath?
         The excuse that thou dost make in this delay
         Is longer than the tale thou dost excuse.
         Is thy news good or bad? Answer to that.   35
         Say either, and I'll stay the circumstance.
         Let me be satisfied, is't good or bad?

NURSE   Well, you have made a simple choice, you know
         not how to choose a man. Romeo? No, not he.
         Though his face be better than any man's, yet   40
         his leg excels all men's; and for a hand, and a
         foot, and a body, though they be not to be talked
         on, yet they are past compare. He is not the
         flower of courtesy, but I'll warrant him, as gentle

123

Eventually the Nurse tells Juliet the arrangement that she is to go to Friar Lawrence's cell to meet Romeo and be married to him.

50	**beats** throbs
52	**Beshrew** Curse
53	**jauncing** travelling busily
59	**within** indoors
63	**hot** impatient
64	**poultice** dressing
66	**coil** to-do
67	**shrift** confession
69	**hie you hence** off you go
71	**wanton ... cheeks** Juliet doesn't want to blush but she can't help herself.
76	**drudge** lowly servant

| | as a lamb. Go thy ways wench, serve God. 45 |
| | What, have you dined at home? |

JULIET   No, no. But all this did I know before.
         What says he of our marriage, what of that?

NURSE   Lord, how my head aches, what a head have I!
         It beats as it would fall in twenty pieces. 50
         My back a t'other side, ah my back, my back!
         Beshrew your heart for sending me about,
         To catch my death with jauncing up and down.

JULIET   I' faith I am sorry that thou art not well.
         Sweet, sweet, sweet Nurse, tell me what says my
               love? 55

NURSE   Your love says, like an honest gentleman, and a
         courteous, and a kind, and a handsome, and I
         warrant a virtuous – Where is your mother?

JULIET   Where is my mother? Why she is within.
         Where should she be? How oddly thou repliest. 60
         'Your love says like an honest gentleman,
         "Where is your mother?"'

NURSE   O God's lady dear,
         Are you so hot? Marry come up I trow,
         Is this the poultice for my aching bones?
         Henceforward do your messages yourself. 65

JULIET   Here's such a coil. Come, what says Romeo?

NURSE   Have you got leave to go to shrift today?

JULIET   I have.

NURSE   Then hie you hence to Friar Lawrence' cell,
         There stays a husband to make you a wife. 70
         Now comes the wanton blood up in your cheeks,
         They'll be in scarlet straight at any news.
         Hie you to church. I must another way,
         To fetch a ladder by the which your love
         Must climb a bird's nest soon when it is dark. 75
         I am the drudge, and toil in your delight.
         But you shall bear the burden soon at night.

Romeo and Friar Lawrence await Juliet's arrival. Romeo is impatient and the Friar tries to persuade him to be patient. Juliet arrives.

1–2   **So smile ... not** May heaven bless this ceremony so that afterwards there is no cause for unhappiness

3   **come what sorrow can** whatever sorrow may come

4   **countervail** equal

9   **These violent ... ends** Extreme emotions such as your love for Juliet often end violently

10   **in their triumph** at the moment of their greatest success

powder gunpowder

11   **Which ... consume** just at the moment when fire and gunpowder touch ('kiss') there is an explosion and they destroy each other

12   **Is loathsome ... deliciousness** can become sickly just because it is so sweet

13   **confounds** destroys

15   **tardy** late

18–19   **bestride ... air** walk on the strands of spiders' web floating in the light summer breeze

21   **ghostly** spiritual

| | Go. I'll to dinner. Hie you to the cell! |
| JULIET | Hie to high fortune! Honest Nurse farewell. |

[Exeunt

Scene 6

Friar Lawrence's cell
Enter FRIAR LAWRENCE *and* ROMEO

F. LAWRENCE	So smile the heavens upon this holy act,
	That after-hours with sorrow chide us not.
ROMEO	Amen, amen, but come what sorrow can,
	It cannot countervail the exchange of joy
	That one short minute gives me in her sight. 5
	Do thou but close our hands with holy words,
	Then love-devouring death do what he dare,
	It is enough I may but call her mine.
F. LAWRENCE	These violent delights have violent ends,
	And in their triumph die, like fire and powder, 10
	Which as they kiss consume. The sweetest honey
	Is loathsome in his own deliciousness,
	And in the taste confounds the appetite.
	Therefore love moderately, long love doth so;
	Too swift arrives as tardy as too slow. 15

Enter JULIET *somewhat fast, and embraceth* ROMEO

	Here comes the lady. O so light a foot
	Will ne'er wear out the everlasting flint.
	A lover may bestride the gossamers
	That idles in the wanton summer air,
	And yet not fall; so light is vanity. 20
JULIET	Good even to my ghostly confessor.
F. LAWRENCE	Romeo shall thank thee daughter for us both.
JULIET	As much to him, else is his thanks too much.

Juliet and Romeo exchange declarations of love. Then the Friar leads them off to be married.

24–5 **measure ... heaped** The idea is of a jug used to measure dry goods like flour. If it is heaped up, you get more than the full measure.

26 **blazon** make public

27 **This neighbour air** this air all around us

27–9 **let rich ... encounter** use your beautiful voice to speak of the inner happiness that we each get from the other in this meeting

30–4 **Conceit ... wealth** Juliet does not like Romeo's extravagant style of speech. She tells him 'True imagination is wealthier in real things than in words and so can talk about reality and not mere decoration. People who can actually count up their wealth are only poor. My own true love has grown so great that I cannot even count up half my wealth.'

ROMEO   Ah, Juliet, if the measure of thy joy
             Be heaped like mine, and that thy skill be more   25
             To blazon it, then sweeten with thy breath
             This neighbour air, and let rich music's tongue
             Unfold the imagined happiness that both
             Receive in either by this dear encounter.

JULIET   Conceit, more rich in matter than in words   30
             Brags of his substance, not of ornament.
             They are but beggars that can count their worth.
             But my true love is grown to such excess,
             I cannot sum up sum of half my wealth.

F. LAWRENCE Come, come with me, and we will make short
                work.   35
             For by your leaves, you shall not stay alone,
             Till holy church incorporate two in one.

                                              [*Exeunt*

In the heat of the day Benvolio and Mercutio are in the street. Benvolio wants Mercutio to withdraw because the Capulets are about and looking for trouble. Mercutio refuses. If anything, he says, Benvolio is the troublemaker.

1	**retire** go back	
2	**the Capels are abroad** the Capulets are out and about	
6	**enters ... tavern** goes inside a public house	
6–7	**claps me his sword** slaps his sword	
8–9	**by the operation ... drawer** under the influence of his second drink draws his sword on the man	
12	**in thy mood** when you get angry	
13–14	**and as soon ... to be moved** as quickly driven to anger and as quickly angry to be so driven	
15	**And what to?** And what would I be driven to?	
16	**and** if (followed by a **play on words** 'to' and 'two')	
22	**hazel** a small sweet nut, and an eye colour	
23	**spy ... quarrel** do his best to find something to quarrel about	
24	**meat** yolk and white	
25	**as addle as an egg** as addled as a rotten egg	

Act Three

Scene 1

Verona. A public place
Enter MERCUTIO, BENVOLIO, *and men*

BENVOLIO   I pray thee good Mercutio, let's retire.
The day is hot, the Capels are abroad,
And if we meet, we shall not 'scape a brawl,
For now these hot days, is the mad blood
stirring.

MERCUTIO   Thou art like one of these fellows that when he   5
enters the confines of a tavern, claps me his
sword upon the table, and says 'God send me
no need of thee;' and by the operation of the
second cup, draws him on the drawer, when
indeed there is no need.   10

BENVOLIO   Am I like such a fellow?

MERCUTIO   Come, come, thou art as hot a Jack in thy mood
as any in Italy, and as soon moved to be moody,
and as soon moody to be moved.

BENVOLIO   And what to?   15

MERCUTIO   Nay and there were two such, we should have
none shortly, for one would kill the other. Thou?
Why thou wilt quarrel with a man that hath a
hair more, or a hair less, in his beard than thou
hast. Thou wilt quarrel with a man for cracking   20
nuts, having no other reason but because thou
hast hazel eyes. What eye, but such an eye,
would spy out such a quarrel? Thy head is as full
of quarrels as an egg is full of meat, and yet thy
head hath been beaten as addle as an egg for   25
quarrelling. Thou hast quarrelled with a man for
coughing in the street, because he hath wakened
thy dog that hath lain asleep in the sun. Didst

Tybalt and his companions approach them, looking for Romeo. Mercutio looks for a fight, while Benvolio urges caution. Romeo arrives.

31   **riband** ribbon (as shoe lace)

33   **apt to quarrel** likely to quarrel

33–5   **any man ... quarter** anyone could buy total possession of my life for an hour and a quarter (because I would soon be dead)

36   **simple** stupid, weak in the head

43   **apt** ready

      an if

46   **consortest** go around with

47   **Consort?** Mercutio takes the word in its other sense, of a group of musicians.

      minstrels travelling musicians

47–9   **An thou ... discords** If you turn us into musicians, be prepared to hear nothing but discords

49   **my fiddlestick** my sword

50   **'Zounds** An oath which comes from the expression 'God's wounds' (a reference to the wounds received by Jesus Christ when he was crucified).

51   **public men** public place

56   **I will not ... pleasure** I'm not going to move to please anyone

57   **my man** the person I am looking for (Mercutio deliberately misunderstands Tybalt and takes him to mean 'my servant'.)

58   **livery** servant's uniform

	thou not fall out with a tailor for wearing his new	
	doublet before Easter? With another for tying his	30
	new shoes with old riband? And yet thou wilt	
	tutor me from quarrelling.	
BENVOLIO	And I were so apt to quarrel as thou art, any	
	man should buy the fee-simple of my life for an	
	hour and a quarter.	35
MERCUTIO	The fee-simple? O simple!	

Enter TYBALT, PETRUCHIO, *and others*

BENVOLIO	By my head, here come the Capulets.	
MERCUTIO	By my heel, I care not.	
TYBALT	Follow me close, for I will speak to them.	
	Gentlemen, good den; a word with one of you.	40
MERCUTIO	And but one word with one of us? Couple it with	
	something, make it a word and a blow.	
TYBALT	You shall find me apt enough to that sir, an you	
	will give me occasion.	
MERCUTIO	Could you not take some occasion without giving?	45
TYBALT	Mercutio, thou consortest with Romeo.	
MERCUTIO	Consort? What, dost thou make us minstrels? An	
	thou make minstrels of us, look to hear nothing	
	but discords. Here's my fiddlestick, here's that	
	shall make you dance. 'Zounds, consort!	50
BENVOLIO	We talk here in the public haunt of men.	
	Either withdraw into some private place,	
	And reason coldly of your grievances,	
	Or else depart; here all eyes gaze on us.	
MERCUTIO	Men's eyes were made to look, and let them	
	gaze.	55
	I will not budge for no man's pleasure, I.	

Enter ROMEO

TYBALT	Well, peace be with you sir, here comes my man.	
MERCUTIO	But I'll be hanged sir, if he wear your livery.	

Tybalt insults Romeo in an attempt to provoke a fight, but Romeo responds calmly and will not take up the challenge. Mercutio is incensed at this apparent cowardice and challenges Tybalt. They fight. Romeo tries to stop the fight and in the confusion Tybalt stabs Mercutio.

59–60 **Marry ... man** You lead the way to the duelling field and he will follow, that's the only sense in which you can call him 'man' (i.e. as a man of honour)

64–5 **excuse ... greeting** allow me to ignore the anger that such a greeting would normally produce

67 **Boy** An insulting form of address.

70 **devise** imagine

72 **tender** hold

75 ***Alla stoccata*** A term from fencing; he deliberately uses one of the foreign technical terms that Tybalt likes to throw around.

76 **rat-catcher** Mercutio is referring to Tybalt's name, which in the story of Reynard the Fox was that of the cat (similar to the modern 'Tibby').

79 **withal** with

80 **as ... hereafter** depending on how you treat me after this

dry-beat beat with a stick

82 **pilcher** scabbard

86 ***passado*** sword thrust (Again he uses one of Tybalt's favourite words and makes fun of him.)

88 **forbear** stop

90 **bandying** quarrelling

	Marry go before to field, he'll be your follower; Your worship in that sense may call him man.	60
TYBALT	Romeo, the love I bear thee can afford No better term than this – thou art a villain.	
ROMEO	Tybalt, the reason that I have to love thee Doth much excuse the appertaining rage To such a greeting. Villain am I none. Therefore farewell, I see thou knowest me not.	65
TYBALT	Boy, this shall not excuse the injuries That thou hast done me, therefore turn and draw.	
ROMEO	I do protest I never injured thee, But love thee better than thou canst devise. Till thou shalt know the reason of my love. And so good Capulet, which name I tender As dearly as mine own, be satisfied.	70
MERCUTIO	O calm, dishonourable, vile submission! *Alla stoccata* carries it away. Tybalt, you rat-catcher, will you walk?	75
TYBALT	What wouldst thou have with me?	
MERCUTIO	Good King of Cats, nothing but one of your nine lives, that I mean to make bold withal, and as you shall use me hereafter, dry-beat the rest of the eight. Will you pluck your sword out of his pilcher by the ears? Make haste, lest mine be about your ears ere it be out.	80
TYBALT	I am for you.	
ROMEO	Gentle Mercutio, put thy rapier up.	85
MERCUTIO	Come sir, your *passado*.	
ROMEO	Draw Benvolio, beat down their weapons. Gentlemen, for shame, forbear this outrage. Tybalt, Mercutio, the Prince expressly hath Forbid this bandying in Verona streets. Hold Tybalt. Good Mercutio.	90
PETRUCHIO	Away Tybalt. [TYBALT *under* ROMEO'S *arm, thrusts* MERCUTIO *in and flies*	

135

As Tybalt and his companions make good their escape, we realise that
Mercutio is fatally wounded. He is helped away but dies almost
immediately.

93	**houses** families (Mercutio is neither a Montague nor a Capulet.)

93   **houses** families (Mercutio is neither a Montague nor a Capulet.)

sped done for

100–1   **a grave man** a **play on words** 1) a serious man (not a joker as previously) 2) buried in a grave

102   **'Zounds** Short for 'God's wounds', a reference to the wounds received by Jesus Christ when he was crucified.

104   **braggart** boaster

104–5   **by ... arithmetic** in modern language 'by the book' (Tybalt has all the technique, but there is no personality to the way he fences. The use of 'arithmetic' also suggests that Tybalt is rather calculating in his behaviour.)

114   **In my behalf** on my account

118   **And in ... steel** weakened the courage in my personality: a **pun** on temper, which can mean 1) state of mind 2) the toughness of steel.

120   **aspired** ascended to

122   **on moe ... depend** threatens more days

MERCUTIO	I am hurt.
	A plague on both your houses, I am sped.
	Is he gone and hath nothing?
BENVOLIO	What, art thou hurt?
MERCUTIO	Ay, ay, a scratch, a scratch, marry 'tis enough. 95
	Where is my page? Go villain, fetch a surgeon.

[Exit Page

ROMEO   Courage man, the hurt cannot be much.

MERCUTIO   No 'tis not so deep as a well, nor so wide as a
             church-door; but 'tis enough, 'twill serve. Ask for
             me tomorrow, and you shall find me a grave   100
             man. I am peppered, I warrant, for this world. A
             plague on both your houses! 'Zounds, a dog, a
             rat, a mouse, a cat, to scratch a man to death!
             A braggart, a rogue, a villain, that fights by the
             book of arithmetic! Why the devil came you   105
             between us? I was hurt under your arm.

ROMEO   I thought all for the best.

MERCUTIO   Help me into some house Benvolio,
             Or I shall faint. A plague on both your houses!
             They have made worms' meat of me. I have it,   110
             And soundly too. Your houses!

[Exeunt MERCUTIO *and* BENVOLIO

ROMEO   This gentleman, the Prince's near ally,
             My very friend, hath got this mortal hurt
             In my behalf; my reputation stained
             With Tybalt's slander. Tybalt that an hour   115
             Hath been my cousin. O sweet Juliet,
             Thy beauty hath made me effeminate,
             And in my temper softened valour's steel.

Enter BENVOLIO

BENVOLIO   O Romeo, Romeo, brave Mercutio is dead.
             That gallant spirit hath aspired the clouds,   120
             Which too untimely here did scorn the earth.

ROMEO   This day's black fate on moe days doth depend,

As Romeo realises what he has done, Tybalt returns. Romeo attacks him frenziedly and kills him. Romeo escapes and the citizens of Verona begin to congregate.

125   **He go ... slain?** Shall I let him go in triumph when Mercutio has been killed?

126   **respective lenity** respectful leniency

127   **fire-eyed ... conduct** In place of mildness Romeo is going to behave with furious anger, eyes blazing.

133   **consort** accompany

137   **doom thee death** sentence you to death

139   **I am fortune's fool** fate (bad luck) has made a fool of me

142   **Up sir** Get up

143   **charge thee** command you

144   **vile ... fray** villains who started this fight

This but begins the woe others must end.

Enter TYBALT.

BENVOLIO	Here comes the furious Tybalt back again.
ROMEO	He go in triumph, and Mercutio slain? 125
	Away to heaven respective lenity,
	And fire-eyed fury be my conduct now.
	Now Tybalt take the 'villain' back again
	That late thou gavest me, for Mercutio's soul
	Is but a little way above our heads, 130
	Staying for thine to keep him company.
	Either thou or I, or both, must go with him.
TYBALT	Thou wretched boy, that didst consort him here,
	Shalt with him hence.
ROMEO	This shall determine that.

[*They fight*. TYBALT *falls*

BENVOLIO	Romeo away, be gone. 135
	The citizens are up and Tybalt slain.
	Stand not amazed, the Prince will doom thee death,
	If thou art taken. Hence, be gone, away.
ROMEO	O I am fortune's fool!
BENVOLIO	Why dost thou stay?

[*Exit* ROMEO

Enter CITIZENS

CITIZEN	Which way ran he that killed Mercutio? 140
	Tybalt, that murderer, which way ran he?
BENVOLIO	There lies that Tybalt.
CITIZEN	Up sir, go with me;
	I charge thee in the Prince's name obey.

Enter PRINCE, MONTAGUE, CAPULET, *their Wives and all*

PRINCE	Where are the vile beginners of this fray?

The Prince questions Benvolio about what happened. Benvolio describes the two fights.

145	**discover** explain
146	**manage** conduct
148	**kinsman** relation
157	**nice** trivial
	and urged withal and in addition warned
160	**take truce** make peace
	unruly spleen hot temper
161	**tilts** makes a thrust
164	**martial scorn** with a soldier's scorn
164–6	**with one ... back** to Tybalt with a dagger in one hand he parries the blow and with his sword returns the blow to Tybalt
167	**Retorts it** sends it back
168	**'Hold ... part!'** Stop and draw apart!
169	**His agile arm** his ready sword
171	**envious** seeking to do evil
174	**had ... revenge** had only just considered revenge
175	**to it they go** they fight
175–6	**ere I could draw** before I could draw my sword
176	**stout** brave

BENVOLIO	O noble Prince, I can discover all 145
	The unlucky manage of this fatal brawl.
	There lies the man, slain by young Romeo,
	That slew thy kinsman, brave Mercutio.
L. CAPULET	Tybalt, my cousin. O my brother's child!
	O Prince! O husband! O the blood is spilled 150
	Of my dear kinsman! Prince, as thou art true,
	For blood of ours shed blood of Montague.
	O cousin, cousin!
PRINCE	Benvolio, who began this bloody fray?
BENVOLIO	Tybalt here slain, whom Romeo's hand did slay. 155
	Romeo, that spoke him fair, bid him bethink
	How nice the quarrel was, and urged withal
	Your high displeasure. All this uttered
	With gentle breath, calm look, knees humbly
	bowed,
	Could not take truce with the unruly spleen 160
	Of Tybalt deaf to peace, but that he tilts
	With piercing steel at bold Mercutio's breast;
	Who, all as hot, turns deadly point to point,
	And with a martial scorn, with one hand beats
	Cold death aside, and with the other sends 165
	It back to Tybalt, whose dexterity
	Retorts it. Romeo he cries aloud,
	'Hold, friends, friends part!' And swifter than his
	tongue,
	His agile arm beats down their fatal points,
	And 'twixt them rushes; underneath whose arm 170
	An envious thrust from Tybalt hit the life
	Of stout Mercutio, and then Tybalt fled;
	But by and by comes back to Romeo,
	Who had but newly entertained revenge,
	And to it they go like lightning, for ere I 175
	Could draw to part them, was stout Tybalt slain.
	And as he fell, did Romeo turn and fly.
	This is the truth, or let Benvolio die.

The Prince pronounces judgement: Romeo is banished and the two families are fined.

180   **Affection** fellow-feeling, friendship (he is a Montague)

186   **Who ... owe?** So who is responsible for Tybalt's death?

188   **His fault ... end** Romeo's killing of Tybalt was perfectly just, and what the law should have achieved

192   **My blood ... a-bleeding** Mercutio was a member of the Prince's family.

193   **amerce** punish

196   **purchase out abuses** buy out these misdeeds

197   **hence** leave Verona

200   **Mercy ... kill** If I show mercy and spare those who kill, I shall only be encouraging murder

L. CAPULET	He is a kinsman to the Montague;
	Affection makes him false, he speaks not true.　180
	Some twenty of them fought in this black strife,
	And all those twenty could but kill one life.
	I beg for justice, which thou, Prince must give.
	Romeo slew Tybalt, Romeo must not live.
PRINCE	Romeo slew him, he slew Mercutio.　185
	Who now the price of his dear blood doth owe?
MONTAGUE	Not Romeo, Prince, he was Mercutio's friend;
	His fault concludes but what the law should end,
	The life of Tybalt.
PRINCE	And for that offence
	Immediately we do exile him hence.　190
	I have an interest in your hate's proceedings;
	My blood for your rude brawls doth lie
	a-bleeding.
	But I'll amerce you with so strong a fine,
	That you shall all repent the loss of mine.
	I will be deaf to pleading and excuses,　195
	Nor tears nor prayers shall purchase out abuses.
	Therefore use none. Let Romeo hence in haste,
	Else, when he is found, that hour is his last.
	Bear hence this body, and attend our will.
	Mercy but murders, pardoning those that kill.　200

[Exeunt

Act 2 scenes 5 and 6; Act 3 scene 1

Themes: youth and age

Act 2 scenes 5 and 6 show us contrasting pictures of youth and age.

Work on your own

1 Copy and complete the table below to collect your thoughts about how Juliet thinks about old people and how she and the Nurse interact in scene 5. It has been started for you.

Lines	Topic	Point	Evidence and explanation
1–17	Juliet's thoughts about the Nurse and old people in general	1. She thinks that the Nurse is being deliberately slow. 2.	1. 'O she is lame': as the messenger of love she should 'fly'.
18–55	How the Nurse treats Juliet's request for news about Romeo		
56–65	How Juliet reacts and the Nurse's response		
66–79	The Nurse's attitude towards Juliet's love for Romeo		

Work with a partner

2 Share your thoughts and add to your tables as needed.

3 Now together draw up a similar table for Act 2 scene 6, describing the behaviour of Friar Lawrence and the ways in which Romeo and Juliet behave towards him.

4 What similarities and differences do you see in the treatment of these two characters?

Performance

There is a lot of dramatic action in Act 3 scene 1. The stage directions tell us when characters enter and exit, but not much more. For example, lines 37–38:

Enter TYBALT, PETRUCHIO, *and others*

BENVOLIO   By my head, here comes the Capulets.

MERCUTIO   By my heel, I care not.

Work on your own

1   Work out your answers to these questions:

    a   How do Tybalt and his friends come in: fast/slow, excited/ calm? Write down some adjectives to describe their entrance.

    b   How do Benvolio and Mercutio react? Do they stand still, move towards Tybalt, move away from him? Do the two of them behave in a similar way or differently from each other?

2   Now look again at lines 39–56. Make notes on the characters' actions:

    a   where they stand in relation to each other

    b   when individuals move

    c   where and how they move.

Work in a group of four or five

3   Share your ideas. Work out an agreed version of the actions in this part of the scene.

4   Cast the parts and rehearse these lines until you are satisfied that they convey the mood and excitement of this confrontation.

5   Now work together to produce a visual description of the scene you have rehearsed. It could be:

    a   a set of movement drawings like those on page 96

    b   a storyboard, like the one on pages 74–5.

Quotation quiz

For each of these quotations, work out:

1 who said it
2 who they were speaking to
3 what it tells us about
   a the speaker
   b the situation.

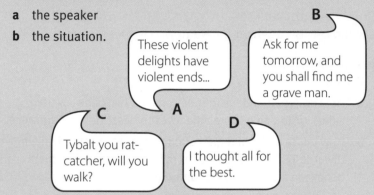

Juliet impatiently awaits the arrival of Romeo.

1–2 **Gallop ... lodging** Phoebus Apollo, the god of the sun, drove his chariot from east to west across the sky. His steeds were fiery-footed. Juliet urges them to gallop fast ('apace') so that night will come and bring Romeo to her.

3 **Phaeton** Apollo's son who was allowed to drive the chariot of the sun for one day but was not strong enough to control it and so the sun came too close to the earth.

9 **if love be blind** Cupid, the god of love, was described in the myths as blind. This idea occurs more than once in the play.

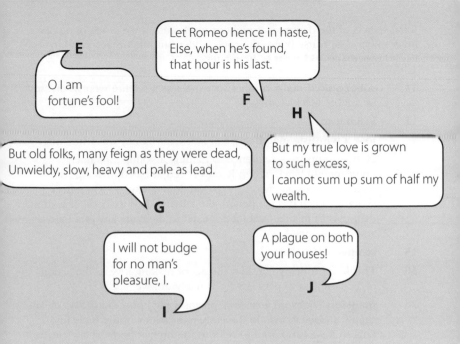

E O I am fortune's fool!

F Let Romeo hence in haste,
Else, when he's found,
that hour is his last.

H But my true love is grown
to such excess,
I cannot sum up sum of half my
wealth.

G But old folks, many feign as they were dead,
Unwieldy, slow, heavy and pale as lead.

I I will not budge
for no man's
pleasure, I.

J A plague on both
your houses!

Scene 2

Juliet's room in Capulet's mansion
Enter JULIET *alone*

JULIET Gallop apace, you fiery-footed steeds,
Towards Phoebus' lodging; such a wagoner
As Phaeton would whip you to the west,
And bring in cloudy night immediately.
Spread thy close curtain, love-performing night, 5
That runaway's eyes may wink, and Romeo
Leap to these arms, untalked of and unseen.
Lovers can see to do their amorous rites
By their own beauties; or if love be blind,
It best agrees with night. Come civil night, 10

Juliet speaks of the darkness of night as her friend, since it will bring her lover to her. The Nurse brings the rope ladder but Juliet is surprised to see her so upset. She asks what is the matter.

11   **sober-suited matron** Juliet sees night as a mature woman dressed in sombre black clothes.

12   **learn** teach

        lose a winning match she will lose her virginity but win Romeo

14–15 **Hood ... mantle** A reference to training a young, untrained ('unmanned') hawk. When it got excited, it bated, making its wings flutter excitedly (as the blood flutters excitedly in Juliet's cheeks). When this happened, the falconer had to 'hood' it with a dark cover ('mantle') until it got used to the company of a man and was 'manned'.

15   **strange** unfamiliar

16   **Think ... modesty** consider the act of making love as the action of a chaste (pure) person who is really in love

26   **mansion** The word 'mansion' means a big house but it also means simply a place to live. In the early translations of the Bible into English it was also used to refer to the human body. Shakespeare probably wants us to have all three meanings in our minds.

27–8   **though ... enjoyed** Juliet says that she, too, is a 'mansion' – again using all three meanings.

37   **weraday** alas

38   **undone** lost, ruined

39   **envious** hostile

Thou sober-suited matron all in black,
And learn me how to lose a winning match,
Played for a pair of stainless maidenhoods.
Hood my unmanned blood, bating in my cheeks,
With thy black mantle, till strange love grown bold,   15
Think true love acted simple modesty.
Come night, come Romeo, come thou day in night;
For thou wilt lie upon the wings of night,
Whiter than new snow upon a raven's back.
Come gentle night, come loving black-browed
    night,   20
Give me my Romeo, and when I shall die,
Take him and cut him out in little stars,
And he will make the face of heaven so fine,
That all the world will be in love with night,
And pay no worship to the garish sun.   25
O I have bought the mansion of a love,
But not possessed it, and, though I am sold,
Not yet enjoyed. So tedious is this day,
As is the night before some festival
To an impatient child that hath new robes   30
And may not wear them. O here comes my Nurse,

Enter NURSE *wringing her hands, with the ladder
of cords in her lap*

And she brings news, and every tongue that speaks
But Romeo's name, speaks heavenly eloquence.
Now Nurse, what news? What hast thou there?
    The cords
That Romeo bid thee fetch?

NURSE   Ay, ay, the cords.   35

JULIET   Ay me, what news? Why dost thou wring thy hands?

NURSE   Ah weraday, he's dead, he's dead, he's dead.
We are undone lady, we are undone.
Alack the day, he's gone, he's killed, he's dead.

JULIET   Can heaven be so envious?

The Nurse is so distressed that she cannot give Juliet a clear reply straight away. At first Juliet is led to believe that it is Romeo who has been killed, but then the Nurse mentions Tybalt's name. At last Juliet discovers the truth that Romeo has been banished for killing Tybalt.

40   **Romeo can** The Nurse means that Romeo could be hostile to Tybalt because he killed him, but Juliet doesn't understand her (since she doesn't know what has happened).

45–50   **'Ay', 'I', eye** (These are all pronounced the same, of course.) In her wild state of mind, Juliet uses a complicated play on words. 'Ay' means 'yes', and was often, in Shakespeare's time, written 'I', a 'bare vowel'. The cockatrice was a mythical creature that could kill you with a look (with its 'eye'). Juliet says that if the answer is 'yes', then she is no longer herself because Romeo's death destroys her true personality. (And if the answer is 'Ay' that he is dead, then his 'eyes' are 'shut'.)

53   **God save the mark** A saying people used to excuse themselves when they were about to say something horrible.

54   **piteous corse** pitiful corpse

56   **swounded** fainted

57   **bankrupt** Her heart has lost all its possessions and so is 'broke'.

59   **Vile earth ... resign** She tells her body ('vile earth') to die (so that it can be buried in the earth).

60   **bier** the stretcher on which the dead body was carried

67   **general doom** On the Day of Judgement the trumpet would sound and all souls called before God to be judged.

73   **serpent** In Genesis, the first book of the Hebrew Bible, the Devil took the form of a snake to tempt Eve in the Garden of Eden.

         flow'ring handsome

NURSE	Romeo can, 40
	Though heaven cannot. O Romeo, Romeo,
	Whoever would have thought it? Romeo!
JULIET	What devil art thou dost torment me thus?
	This torture should be roared in dismal hell.
	Hath Romeo slain himself? Say thou but 'Ay', 45
	And that bare vowel 'I' shall poison more
	Than the death-darting eye of cockatrice.
	I am not I, if there be such an 'I';
	Or those eyes shut, that makes thee answer 'Ay'.
	If he be slain, say 'ay'; or if not, 'no'. 50
	Brief sounds determine of my weal or woe.
NURSE	I saw the wound, I saw it with mine eyes –
	God save the mark – here on his manly breast.
	A piteous corse, a bloody piteous corse,
	Pale, pale as ashes, all bedaubed in blood, 55
	All in gore-blood. I swounded at the sight.
JULIET	O break, my heart, poor bankrupt, break at once.
	To prison eyes, ne'er look on liberty.
	Vile earth, to earth resign; end motion here;
	And thou and Romeo press one heavy bier. 60
NURSE	O Tybalt, Tybalt, the best friend I had,
	O courteous Tybalt, honest gentleman,
	That ever I should live to see thee dead!
JULIET	What storm is this that blows so contrary?
	Is Romeo slaughtered? And is Tybalt dead? 65
	My dearest cousin, and my dearer lord?
	Then dreadful trumpet, sound the general doom,
	For who is living, if those two are gone?
NURSE	Tybalt is gone, and Romeo banished.
	Romeo that killed him, he is banished. 70
JULIET	O God, did Romeo's hand shed Tybalt's blood?
NURSE	It did, it did, alas the day, it did!
JULIET	O serpent heart, hid with a flow'ring face!
	Did ever dragon keep so fair a cave?

Juliet is distraught at her conflict of loyalties: she loves Romeo but he has killed her cousin. When the Nurse tries to comfort her by agreeing and criticising Romeo, Juliet turns on her.

75–7 **Beautiful ... show** Juliet has two ideas in her mind: (a) that the Devil was once an angel who rebelled against God and so was once beautiful (b) that Romeo appears beautiful but his beauty hides an evil soul (because he killed Tybalt). These are further examples of **oxymoron** (see Glossary p. 291).

78 **Just** exact

81–2 **bower ... flesh** house the soul of a devil in such a beautiful and apparently saintly body

83–4 **Was ever ... bound?** This reminds us of the way her mother described Paris (look at the top of p. 51), but Juliet is saying something very different.

86–7 **perjured/forsworn/dissemblers** all words referring to people who have lied about the most important things in life

87 **naught** nothing

88 **aqua vitae** brandy

95 **chide at** criticise

98 **smooth** make whole

99 **mangled** cut it to bits

102–4 **Back ... joy** She tells her tears to go back where they came from since they should be paying tribute to sadness and not, as they are, being shed for happiness (her happiness that Romeo is still alive).

Beautiful tyrant, fiend angelical,   75
Dove-feathered raven, wolvish-ravening lamb,
Despised substance of divinest show,
Just opposite to what thou justly seem'st,
A damned saint, an honourable villain.
O nature, what hadst thou to do in hell,   80
When thou didst bower the spirit of a fiend
In mortal paradise of such sweet flesh?
Was ever book containing such vile matter
So fairly bound? O that deceit should dwell
In such a gorgeous palace!

NURSE   There's no trust,   85
No faith, no honesty in men; all perjured,
All forsworn, all naught, all dissemblers.
Ah, where's my man? Give me some aqua vitae.
These griefs, these woes, these sorrows make
   me old.
Shame come to Romeo.

JULIET   Blistered be thy tongue   90
For such a wish. He was not born to shame.
Upon his brow shame is ashamed to sit;
For 'tis a throne where honour may be crowned
Sole monarch of the universal earth.
O what a beast was I to chide at him!   95

NURSE   Will you speak well of him that killed your cousin?

JULIET   Shall I speak ill of him that is my husband?
Ah poor my lord, what tongue shall smooth thy
   name,
When I thy three-hours' wife have mangled it?
But wherefore villain didst thou kill my cousin?   100
That villain cousin would have killed my
   husband.
Back foolish tears, back to your native spring.
Your tributary drops belong to woe,
Which you mistaking offer up to joy.
My husband lives, that Tybalt would have slain,   105
And Tybalt's dead, that would have slain my
   husband.

Juliet is even more upset when she begins to realise what Romeo's banishment means to her. The Nurse says that she will go to Romeo, who is hiding at Friar Lawrence's cell.

107   **wherefore ... then?** so why am I crying?

109   **forget it fain** gladly forget it

112   **banished** The third syllable is pronounced (to rhyme with 'head'.)

114   **Hath slain** would be enough to have killed ten thousand Tybalts

116–20 Or if ... moved? Or if unhappiness has to have company why didn't the death of her mother or father (or both) follow on from Tybalt's? That would have been an ordinary ('modern') kind of grief

121   **with a rear-ward following** following on from

122–4   **to speak ... dead!** if you say that, then it's as good as killing father, mother, Tybalt, Romeo and me – all of us!

126   **that word's death** the death that word can cause

132   **beguiled** cheated

135   **maiden-widowed** made a widow before the wedding night

137   **maidenhead** virginity

139   **wot** know

All this is comfort, wherefore weep I then?
Some word there was, worser than Tybalt's death,
That murdered me. I would forget it fain;
But O it presses to my memory,   110
Like damned guilty deeds to sinners' minds.
'Tybalt is dead, and Romeo banished.'
That 'banished', that one word 'banished',
Hath slain ten thousand Tybalts. Tybalt's death
Was woe enough if it had ended there.   115
Or if sour woe delights in fellowship,
And needly will be ranked with other griefs,
Why followed not, when she said, 'Tybalt's dead',
'Thy father', or 'thy mother', nay or both,
Which modern lamentation might have moved?   120
But with a rear-ward following Tybalt's death,
'Romeo is banished' – to speak that word,
Is father, mother, Tybalt, Romeo, Juliet,
All slain, all dead! 'Romeo is banished.'
There is no end, no limit, measure, bound,   125
In that word's death; no words can that woe sound.
Where is my father and my mother, Nurse?

NURSE   Weeping and wailing over Tybalt's corse.
Will you go to them? I will bring you thither.

JULIET   Wash they his wounds with tears? Mine shall be
        spent,   130
When theirs are dry, for Romeo's banishment.
Take up those cords. Poor ropes you are beguiled,
Both you and I, for Romeo is exiled.
He made you for a highway to my bed,
But I a maid die maiden-widowed.   135
Come cords, come Nurse, I'll to my wedding-bed,
And death, not Romeo, take my maidenhead.

NURSE   Hie to your chamber. I'll find Romeo
To comfort you. I wot well where he is.
Hark ye, your Romeo will be here at night.   140
I'll to him, he is hid at Lawrence' cell.

Juliet sends her ring as a token and asks the Nurse to tell Romeo to come to her to say goodbye.

Friar Lawrence returns to his cell, where Romeo is hiding. He tells Romeo that the Prince's sentence is banishment from Verona. Romeo responds that since he will no longer be able to be with Juliet, it might as well be a death sentence.

1	**fearful** frightened	
2–3	**Affliction ... calamity** Unhappiness has fallen in love with you, and you are married to disaster	
4	**doom** sentence	
5	**What sorrow ... hand** What new unhappiness wants to get to know me	
9	**doomsday** the Last Judgement when it is decided whether our soul will enter Heaven or Hell	
18	**purgatory** where the souls of the dead were purged (cleansed) of sin before they could enter Heaven	
	torture Purgatory was expected to be painful but in Hell souls were tortured forever.	
21	**death mis-termed** another name for death	

JULIET	O find him, give this ring to my true knight,
	And bid him come to take his last farewell.

[Exeunt

Scene 3

Friar Lawrence's cell
Enter FRIAR LAWRENCE

F. LAWRENCE	Romeo come forth, come forth thou fearful man.
	Affliction is enamoured of thy parts,
	And thou art wedded to calamity.

Enter ROMEO

ROMEO	Father what news? What is the Prince's doom?	
	What sorrow craves acquaintance at my hand,	5
	That I yet know not?	
F. LAWRENCE	Too familiar	
	Is my dear son with such sour company.	
	I bring thee tidings of the Prince's doom.	
ROMEO	What less than doomsday is the Prince's doom?	
F. LAWRENCE	A gentler judgement vanished from his lips,	10
	Not body's death, but body's banishment.	
ROMEO	Ha, banishment? Be merciful, say 'death';	
	For exile hath more terror in his look,	
	Much more than death. Do not say 'banishment'.	
F. LAWRENCE	Hence from Verona art thou banished.	15
	Be patient, for the world is broad and wide.	
ROMEO	There is no world without Verona walls,	
	But purgatory, torture, hell itself.	
	Hence banished is banished from the world,	
	And world's exile is death. Then 'banished'	20
	Is death mis-termed. Calling death 'banished',	

As Romeo speaks he becomes increasingly wild and repeats that he might as well be dead.

24	**rude** ignorant, rough, uncivilised
25	**Thy fault ... death** According to our law, the penalty for what you have done is death
26	**rushed aside** pushed to one side
29	**Heaven** Romeo's thoughts continue to focus on religious themes. When he first spoke to Juliet he thought of her as a saint (p. 69 lines 92–3).
33–5	**More validity ... Romeo** Blowflies are more valued, respected and honoured than Romeo
	validity value
35	**carrion flies** flies that feed on dead flesh
38	**vestal** virgin
39	**Still ... sin** His idea is that her lips blush when they touch (kiss) each other.
45	**No sudden mean ... mean** no method of instant killing, however wretched
47	**the damned ... hell** Souls that are in hell are banished from the presence of God.
49	**divine** man of the church
	ghostly spiritual
50	**sin-absolver** his confessor who pronounces forgiveness of his sins
51	**mangle** hack, cut repeatedly
52	**fond** foolish
55	**Adversity's ... philosophy** when everything seems to be against you it will help to be philosophical

	Thou cut'st my head off with a golden axe,	
	And smilest upon the stroke that murders me.	
F. LAWRENCE	O deadly sin! O rude unthankfulness!	
	Thy fault our law calls death, but the kind Prince	25
	Taking thy part hath rushed aside the law,	
	And turned that black word death to banishment.	
	This is dear mercy, and thou seest it not.	
ROMEO	'Tis torture and not mercy. Heaven is here	
	Where Juliet lives, and every cat and dog,	30
	And little mouse, every unworthy thing,	
	Live here in heaven, and may look on her,	
	But Romeo may not. More validity,	
	More honourable state, more courtship lives	
	In carrion flies than Romeo. They may seize	35
	On the white wonder of dear Juliet's hand,	
	And steal immortal blessing from her lips,	
	Who even in pure and vestal modesty	
	Still blush, as thinking their own kisses sin.	
	But Romeo may not, he is banished.	40
	Flies may do this, but I from this must fly;	
	They are free men, but I am banished.	
	And sayest thou yet that exile is not death?	
	Hadst thou no poison mixed, no sharp-ground knife,	
	No sudden mean of death, though ne'er so mean,	45
	But 'banished' to kill me? Banished?	
	O Friar, the damned use that word in hell;	
	Howling attends it. How hast thou the heart,	
	Being a divine, a ghostly confessor,	
	A sin-absolver, and my friend professed,	50
	To mangle me with that word banished?	
F. LAWRENCE	Thou fond mad man, hear me a little speak.	
ROMEO	O thou wilt speak again of banishment.	
F. LAWRENCE	I'll give thee armour to keep off that word,	
	Adversity's sweet milk, philosophy,	55
	To comfort thee though thou art banished.	

Romeo continues to reject the Friar's advice. Their conversation is interrupted by someone knocking at the door.

57   **Hang up philosophy** Philosophy be hanged

59   **Displant a town** shift Verona somewhere else

        reverse a prince's doom overturn a prince's condemnation

60   **it prevails not** it can't win

64   **that** what

66   **An hour but married** only married just an hour ago

67   **Doting like me** as love-sick as I am

70   **Taking ... grave** measuring my grave which hasn't yet been dug

71   **Arise** Get up

72–3   **Not I ... eyes** Romeo is refusing to hide, but suggests that heaving heavy love-sick groans might create a mist to hide him.

75   **Stay awhile** Wait just a moment (to the Nurse)

76   **By and by** I'll open in a moment

77   **simpleness** foolish behaviour

ROMEO   Yet 'banished'? Hang up philosophy,
                 Unless philosophy can make a Juliet,
                 Displant a town, reverse a prince's doom,
                 It helps not, it prevails not. Talk no more.   60

F. LAWRENCE   O then I see that madmen have no ears.

ROMEO   How should they when that wise men have no eyes?

F. LAWRENCE   Let me dispute with thee of thy estate.

ROMEO   Thou canst not speak of that thou dost not feel.
                 Wert thou as young as I, Juliet thy love,   65
                 An hour but married, Tybalt murdered,
                 Doting like me, and like me banished,
                 Then mightst thou speak, then mightst thou tear
                     thy hair,
                 And fall upon the ground, as I do now,
                 Taking the measure of an unmade grave.   70

                 NURSE *knocks*

F. LAWRENCE   Arise; one knocks; good Romeo hide thyself.

ROMEO   Not I, unless the breath of heart-sick groans
                 Mist-like enfold me from the search of eyes.
                                           [NURSE *knocks*

F. LAWRENCE   Hark how they knock! Who's there? Romeo, arise;
                 Thou wilt be taken – Stay awhile – Stand up.   75
                                           [NURSE *knocks*
                 Run to my study – By and by – God's will,
                 What simpleness is this? – I come, I come.
                                           [NURSE *knocks*
                 Who knocks so hard? Whence come you? What's
                 your will?

NURSE   [*Within*] Let me come in, and you shall know my
                     errand.
                 I come from Lady Juliet.

F. LAWRENCE   Welcome then.   80

NURSE   O holy Friar, o tell me holy Friar,

The Nurse arrives to see Romeo collapsed on the floor in his unhappiness. She tells them that Juliet is similarly grief-stricken. On hearing this Romeo blames himself and tries to kill himself but they stop him.

84   **O he ... case** he is in just the same state as my mistress

85   **woeful sympathy** Romeo and Juliet are sharing the same misery.

86   **Piteous predicament!** such a pitiful state!

88   **an you be** if you are

90   **so deep an O** such a deep groan

93   **an old murderer** a habitual murderer

95   **With ... own** I have killed a relation of hers

97   **My concealed lady** my secret wife

101   **that name** Romeo uses his name to refer to himself.

102   **level** aim

105–6   **In what ... lodge?** in which evil part of my body does my name live?

106   **sack** destroy

107–12 **Hold ... both** Romeo is prevented from stabbing himself and the Friar scolds him for his tears and his wildness, more like that of an animal which cannot use reason than a proper young man.

	Where's my lady's lord? Where's Romeo?
F. LAWRENCE	There on the ground, with his own tears made drunk.

NURSE
O he is even in my mistress' case,
Just in her case. O woeful sympathy,   85
Piteous predicament! Even so lies she,
Blubbering and weeping, weeping and
    blubbering.
Stand up, stand up; stand an you be a man.
For Juliet's sake, for her sake rise and stand.
Why should you fall into so deep an O?   90

ROMEO
Nurse –

NURSE
            Ah sir, ah sir, death's the end of all.

ROMEO
Spakest thou of Juliet? How is it with her?
Doth she not think me an old murderer,
Now I have stained the childhood of our joy
With blood removed but little from her own?   95
Where is she? And how doth she? And what says
My concealed lady to our cancelled love?

NURSE
O she says nothing sir, but weeps and weeps,
And now falls on her bed, and then starts up,
And Tybalt calls, and then on Romeo cries,   100
And then down falls again.

ROMEO
                                    As if that name,
Shot from the deadly level of a gun,
Did murder her, as that name's cursed hand
Murdered her kinsman. O tell me Friar, tell me,
In what vile part of this anatomy   105
Doth my name lodge? Tell me that I may sack
The hateful mansion.
[*He offers to stab himself and* NURSE *snatches the
    dagger awa*y

F. LAWRENCE
                                    Hold thy desperate hand.
Art thou a man? Thy form cries out thou art.
Thy tears are womanish, thy wild acts denote
The unreasonable fury of a beast.   110
Unseemly woman in a seeming man,

Friar Lawrence tells him to get control of himself: Juliet and he are both still alive.

113–14 Thou ... tempered The Friar is horrified at the character that Romeo is revealing.

116 that ... lives whose life depends on yours

117 doing ... thyself committing suicide: it was believed that anyone who committed suicide was damned and would go to hell.

118 Why railest thou on Why do you abuse

119–20 all three ... thee at once all these come together in your body

120 at once wouldst lose suddenly want to destroy

121–4 Fie, fie ... thy wit The Friar compares Romeo to a man lending money in order to make money by charging interest. He claims this is not a proper use of money and Romeo is misusing his own person, his love of Juliet and his reason.

125 form of wax a wax image, not flesh and blood and intellect

126 Digressing ... man departing from the personality of a man

127 hollow perjury a false oath

129–33 Thy wit ... defence The Friar tells Romeo that his present lack of intelligent reasoning, because of his passion, puts him in danger. He compares him to an unskilled soldier who, instead of using his gun for his defence, manages to blow himself up by setting light to the gunpowder.

135 dead wanting to die

136 would wanted to

141 Happiness ... array happiness woos (makes up to) you all dressed in its best clothes

142 mishaved badly behaved

sullen wench bad-tempered girl

144 such die miserable people who behave in that way die unhappy

145 decreed arranged

147 the watch be set At night the gates of the city were closed and the streets patrolled by watchmen. So Romeo could either leave freely before then, or early the following morning in disguise, as soon as the gates were opened again.

And ill-beseeming beast in seeming both,
Thou hast amazed me. By my holy order,
I thought thy disposition better tempered.
Hast thou slain Tybalt? Wilt thou slay thyself,   115
And slay thy lady that in thy life lives,
By doing damned hate upon thyself?
Why railest thou on thy birth, the heaven, and earth,
Since birth, and heaven, and earth, all three do
     meet
In thee at once; which thou at once wouldst lose?   120
Fie, fie, thou shamest thy shape, thy love, thy wit,
Which like a usurer abound'st in all,
And usest none in that true use indeed
Which should bedeck thy shape, thy love, thy wit.
Thy noble shape is but a form of wax,   125
Digressing from the valour of a man;
Thy dear love sworn but hollow perjury,
Killing that love which thou hast vowed to cherish.
Thy wit, that ornament to shape and love,
Misshapen in the conduct of them both,   130
Like powder in a skilless soldier's flask,
Is set afire by thine own ignorance,
And thou dismembered with thine own defence.
What, rouse thee man, thy Juliet is alive,
For whose dear sake thou wast but lately dead.   135
There art thou happy. Tybalt would kill thee,
But thou slewest Tybalt; there art thou happy.
The law that threatened death becomes thy friend,
And turns it to exile; there art thou happy.
A pack of blessings light upon thy back,   140
Happiness courts thee in her best array,
But like a mishaved and sullen wench,
Thou pouts upon thy fortune and thy love.
Take heed, take heed, for such die miserable.
Go get thee to thy love as was decreed,   145
Ascend her chamber, hence and comfort her.
But look thou stay not till the watch be set,

Romeo must go to Mantua and wait until the situation can be sorted out. The Nurse gives Romeo Juliet's ring and they arrange that Romeo will spend the night with Juliet but depart for Mantua before it is light.

150   **blaze** make public

153   **lamentation** grief

156   **Which heavy ... unto** which they are likely to want to do anyway because of their grief

159   **counsel** advice

161   **bid ... chide** tell my love to prepare to blame me

162   **bid me** told me

163   **Hie you** Hurry

164   **my comfort is revived** I am very relieved

165   **here ... state** your whole future depends on your going

166   **before ... set** a night watchman would be posted, and the city gates closed

167   **disguised from hence** If Romeo spends the night with Juliet he will have to leave in disguise in the morning.

168–70 Sojourn ... here The Friar tells Romeo to stay in Mantua for the time being and promises to contact Romeo's servant and use him to carry news of what is happening in Verona.

172–3 But ... thee If it were not that such a great joy draws me away, I would be sad to part from you so hurriedly

For then thou canst not pass to Mantua,
Where thou shalt live till we can find a time
To blaze your marriage, reconcile your friends,   150
Beg pardon of the Prince, and call thee back
With twenty hundred thousand times more joy
Than thou went'st forth in lamentation.
Go before Nurse, commend me to thy lady,
And bid her hasten all the house to bed,   155
Which heavy sorrow makes them apt unto.
Romeo is coming.

NURSE   O Lord, I could have stayed here all the night
               to hear good counsel. O what learning is!
               My lord, I'll tell my lady you will come.   160

ROMEO   Do so, and bid my sweet prepare to chide.
                         [NURSE *offers to go in and turns again*

NURSE   Here sir, a ring she bid me give you sir.
               Hie you, make haste, for it grows very late.
                                                      [*Exit*

ROMEO   How well my comfort is revived by this.

F. LAWRENCE   Go hence; good night; and here stands all your
                         state —   165
               Either be gone before the watch be set,
               Or by the break of day disguised from hence.
               Sojourn in Mantua; I'll find out your man,
               And he shall signify from time to time
               Every good hap to you that chances here.   170
               Give me thy hand, 'tis late. Farewell; good night.

ROMEO   But that a joy past joy calls out on me,
               It were a grief, so brief to part with thee.
               Farewell.
                                                      [*Exeunt*

Juliet's father, Capulet, tells Paris that he agrees to his marriage to Juliet. The ceremony shall take place two and a half days later, on Thursday. Lady Capulet will tell Juliet what they have decided.

1	**fall'n out** happened	
2	**move** make a proposal to	
6	**but for** if I had not had	
9	**commend me** present my greetings	
10	**know her mind** have her decision	
11	**mewed ... heaviness** shut up with her grief	
12	**desperate tender** bold offer	
16	**son** Paris will be his son-in-law, but this is polite anticipation.	
17	**bid ... me** tell her, listen well	
18	**soft** wait a moment	
19	**Ha, ha** Hm, hm (these are considering noises, not laughter)	
20	**a** on	
23	**We'll ... ado** We won't make much fuss	
24	**hark you** listen	
	late recently	
25–6	**It may ... much** people might consider that we thought little of him if we hold great celebrations	

Scene ❹

Capulet's mansion
Enter CAPULET, LADY CAPULET, *and* PARIS

CAPULET Things have fall'n out sir, so unluckily,
That we have had no time to move our daughter.
Look you, she loved her kinsman Tybalt dearly,
And so did I. Well, we were born to die.
'Tis very late, she'll not come down tonight.   5
I promise you, but for your company,
I would have been abed an hour ago.

PARIS These times of woe afford no time to woo.
Madam good night, commend me to your
daughter.

L. CAPULET I will, and know her mind early tomorrow;   10
Tonight she's mewed up to her heaviness.
[PARIS *offers to go in and* CAPULET *calls him again*

CAPULET Sir Paris, I will make a desperate tender
Of my child's love. I think she will be ruled
In all respects by me; nay more, I doubt it not.
Wife, go you to her ere you go to bed,   15
Acquaint her here of my son Paris' love;
And bid her, mark you me, on Wednesday next –
But soft, what day is this?

PARIS   Monday my lord.

CAPULET Monday? Ha ha, well Wednesday is too soon;
A Thursday let it be a Thursday, tell her,   20
She shall be married to this noble earl.
Will you be ready? Do you like this haste?
We'll keep no great ado – a friend or two.
For hark you, Tybalt being slain so late,
It may be thought we held him carelessly,   25
Being our kinsman, if we revel much.
Therefore we'll have some half a dozen friends,
And there an end. But what say you to Thursday?

169

32	**against** in anticipation of
34	**Afore me** The servant should go ahead with the light.
35	**by and by** in a minute

Act 3 scenes 2, 3 and 4

'Now Nurse, what news?'

Act 3 scene 2 begins with Juliet eagerly anticipating her wedding night. But we know already that things have gone very badly wrong and that Romeo has been banished. This is an example of dramatic irony, where the audience knows more than the characters on stage. This scene shows Juliet gradually discovering the truth that we already know, step by step.

Work on your own

1   The table opposite highlights the main steps in that process. Copy it out and fill in the gaps; it has been started for you.

Work with a partner

2   Compare your ideas and add to your table, or change it where necessary.

3   Choose two sections next to each other (for example, lines 52–60 and 61–8). Cast the two parts and read the lines aloud. Concentrate on getting across Juliet's confusion and the way in which her thoughts change as you cross the line between the two sections.

PARIS   My lord, I would that Thursday were tomorrow.

CAPULET   Well get you gone; a' Thursday be it then.   30
         Go you to Juliet ere you go to bed,
         Prepare her, wife, against this wedding-day.
         Farewell my lord. Light to my chamber ho!
         Afore me, it is so very late that we
         May call it early by and by. Good night.   35
                                              [*Exeunt*

Lines	Summary of what Juliet is thinking	Key words or expressions
1–35		
36–51	Is Romeo dead, then? Has he killed himself?	'Hath Romeo slain himself?' 'If he be slain, say "ay"; or if not, "no".'
52–60		
61–8		
69–85		
86–95		
96–111		
112–26		
127–37		

'Thou fond mad man'

Romeo

The Friar is certainly not impressed with Romeo in Act 3 scene 3. He calls him a 'fond (*foolish*) mad man' – and that is *before* Romeo threatens himself with a dagger. How should we feel about Romeo?

Here are some words that we might use about Romeo's behaviour during this scene:

self-pitying	arrogant	selfish
childish	sulky	thoughtful
grateful	brave	attention-seeking

Work in a group of three

1 Decide which three of the words above best sum up what Romeo is like in this scene.

2 For each word you have chosen, find one point in the scene that clearly shows Romeo behaving in that way. (Each point should be one or two lines in the text.)

3 One of you should play Romeo. The other two should: help Romeo strike a suitable pose at each chosen point. Try to make each pose express the word chosen for that point.

4 Show your series of poses to another group. Ask them to work out which behaviour words you are trying to express.

5 Now try speaking the lines at the chosen points in the scene, still trying to express the chosen behaviour words.

Manliness

The Friar tells Romeo, 'Thy tears are womanish' (line 109). Clearly the Friar associates manliness with emotional self-control.

Work on your own

1 Find three other references in this scene to how men ought to behave. You could look at the speeches that start on lines 84 and 107.

2 For each reference you find, explain in about 20 words what it shows about attitudes towards men and women.

'Tell her, she shall be married'

Act 3 scene 4 is a short scene but it packs a lot in. It is also a puzzling scene that raises some interesting questions. If you were producing the play you would have to find answers to these questions.

What is the background?

Work in a group of three

1 Work out your answers to these questions:

    a When does the scene take place? (Look at lines 33–5.)

    b Why is Paris there at this time? Remember that everyone knows that a member of the Capulet family has just been killed in a fight.

    c Why is Capulet so keen on seeing Paris and talking about him marrying Juliet? Why doesn't he just tell him to go away and come back at a more suitable time?

2 The scene starts in the middle of a conversation. Think about what Paris, Capulet, and Lady Capulet might have been saying to each other before it begins.

    a Cast the parts.

    b Improvise this conversation.

What do we feel about Tybalt's death? (lines 1–11)

3 Look carefully at lines 3–4. Discuss:

    a what they tell us about Capulet's true feelings

    b how these lines should be spoken to get this across.

4 Each try saying the lines until you are satisfied you have got them right.

5 Now read lines 1–11 aloud.

Why the hurry? (lines 12–21)

6 Work out your answers to these questions:

    a Lady Capulet has said they will talk to Juliet about the wedding the next day, and Paris seems happy with that (lines 10–11). Just as Paris is leaving, Capulet 'calls him again', and speaks lines 12–14. Why the hurry?

   b What do you think this tells us about Capulet and his reasons for wanting Paris as a son-in-law?

   c What does it tell us about Capulet's attitude towards Juliet?

   d If you read lines 17 and 21, what does this add to your impression of how Capulet thinks of his daughter?

7 Now read lines 12–21 aloud. In your reading try to get across what you have decided about Capulet.

What difference does a day make? (lines 22–9)

8 Work out your answers to these questions.

   a Why does Capulet change the wedding day from Wednesday to Thursday?

   b Do you think this makes sense?

   c What does it tell us about him?

   d How sincere is his grief at the death of Tybalt? Why do you think this?

9 Now work on a reading of lines 22–9 to communicate these ideas.

Orders, orders, orders

10 At the end of the scene Capulet is on a high, telling everyone what to do. Look at how he speaks to:

   a Paris

   b his wife

   c his servant.

Discuss how these orders should be delivered: fast or slow? quiet or loud?

11 Work on a reading of this speech to get these ideas across.

The whole scene

12 You have now explored the scene and answered the main questions it raises, section by section. What does this scene tell us about:

   a the character of Capulet

   b his relationships with the other characters?

Quotation quiz

For each of these quotations, work out:

1 who said it
2 who they were speaking to
3 what it tells us about
    a the speaker
    b the situation.

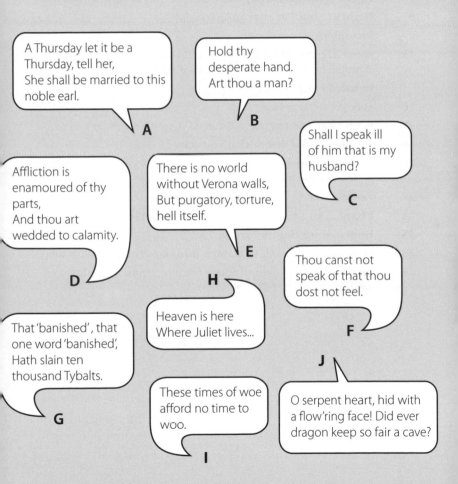

A Thursday let it be a Thursday, tell her, She shall be married to this noble earl.

A

Hold thy desperate hand. Art thou a man?

B

Shall I speak ill of him that is my husband?

C

Affliction is enamoured of thy parts, And thou art wedded to calamity.

D

There is no world without Verona walls, But purgatory, torture, hell itself.

E

Thou canst not speak of that thou dost not feel.

F

That 'banished', that one word 'banished', Hath slain ten thousand Tybalts.

G

Heaven is here Where Juliet lives...

H

These times of woe afford no time to woo.

I

O serpent heart, hid with a flow'ring face! Did ever dragon keep so fair a cave?

J

It is almost light and Romeo is preparing to leave Juliet and travel to Mantua. Juliet tries to persuade him to stay, saying that it is still night and Romeo says he will accept her judgement and risk death. Juliet realises he was right before and tells him he must go.

3   **fearful** apprehensive, worried about what is going to happen

4   **yon** yonder, over there

7   **envious** spiteful

7–8   **envious ... east** the first spiteful streaks of light are parting the clouds in the eastern sky

9   **Night's ... out** The stars are going out

        jocund happy

13   **some ... exhaled** People believed that meteors were sucked up from the earth by the sun which then set them on fire.

        exhaled breathed out

16   **stay yet** still stay here

17   **ta'en** taken (said as one syllable, to rhyme with 'main')

18   **so thou ... so** if that is what you want

20   **the pale ... brow** the pale reflection of the forehead of Cynthia, goddess of the moon

22   **vaulty** domed

23   **I have ... go** I want to stay more than I want to go

25   **How ... soul?** How are you, my love?

28   **Straining** forcing out (but also a **pun** on 'strain', meaning 'tune')

29   **division** a run of musical notes (but also a **pun** – see the next line)

Scene ⑤

Juliet's bedroom
Enter ROMEO, *and* JULIET *at the window*

JULIET Wilt thou be gone? It is not yet near day.
   It was the nightingale, and not the lark,
   That pierced the fearful hollow of thine ear;
   Nightly she sings on yon pomegranate tree.
   Believe me love, it was the nightingale.   5

ROMEO It was the lark, the herald of the morn,
   No nightingale. Look love, what envious streaks
   Do lace the severing clouds in yonder east.
   Night's candles are burnt out, and jocund day
   Stands tiptoe on the misty mountain tops.   10
   I must be gone and live, or stay and die.

JULIET Yon light is not daylight, I know it, I.
   It is some meteor that the sun exhaled,
   To be to thee this night a torch-bearer,
   And light thee on thy way to Mantua.   15
   Therefore stay yet, thou need'st not to be gone.

ROMEO Let me be ta'en, let me be put to death;
   I am content, so thou wilt have it so.
   I'll say yon grey is not the morning's eye,
   'Tis but the pale reflex of Cynthia's brow.   20
   Nor that is not the lark, whose notes do beat
   The vaulty heaven so high above our heads.
   I have more care to stay than will to go.
   Come death, and welcome, Juliet wills it so.
   How is't, my soul? Let's talk; it is not day.   25

JULIET It is, it is, hie hence, be gone, away.
   It is the lark that sings so out of tune,
   Straining harsh discords, and unpleasing sharps.
   Some say the lark makes sweet division;

The Nurse warns them that Lady Capulet is coming and Romeo and Juliet say farewell. Romeo leaves.

31 **Some ... eyes** Because a toad's eyes are more beautiful than a lark's

33–4 **Since ... day** since that noise startles us out of each other's arms, chasing you away with the morning call that wakes the hunters

36 **More light ... woes** The lighter it gets, the sadder we become

52–3 **all these ... discourses** all these sadnesses will form the subject of our conversation

54 **ill-divining** fearing that something bad will happen in the future

55 **now ... low** because Romeo has started climbing down the ladder

59 **Dry ... blood** People believed that sighing (for sorrow) thinned your blood and so made you pale.

60 **fickle** changeable, unreliable

	This doth not so, for she divideth us.	30
	Some say the lark and loathed toad change eyes,	
	O now I would they had changed voices too,	
	Since arm from arm that voice doth us affray,	
	Hunting thee hence with hunt's-up to the day.	
	O now be gone; more light and light it grows.	35
ROMEO	More light and light, more dark and dark our woes.	

Enter NURSE *hastily*

NURSE	Madam.	
JULIET	Nurse.	
NURSE	Your lady mother is coming to your chamber.	
	The day is broke, be wary, look about.	40

[*Exit*

| JULIET | Then window let day in, and let life out. | |
| ROMEO | Farewell, farewell. One kiss, and I'll descend. | |

[*He goes down*

JULIET	Art thou gone so, love lord, ay husband, friend?	
	I must hear from thee every day in the hour,	
	For in a minute there are many days.	45
	O by this count I shall be much in years,	
	Ere I again behold my Romeo.	
ROMEO	Farewell.	
	I will omit no opportunity	
	That may convey my greetings, love, to thee.	50
JULIET	O think'st thou we shall ever meet again?	
ROMEO	I doubt it not, and all these woes shall serve	
	For sweet discourses in our time to come.	
JULIET	O God, I have an ill-divining soul.	
	Methinks I see thee now thou art so low,	55
	As one dead in the bottom of a tomb.	
	Either my eyesight fails, or thou lookest pale.	
ROMEO	And trust me love, in my eye so do you.	
	Dry sorrow drinks our blood. Adieu, adieu.	

[*Exit*

| JULIET | O fortune, fortune, all men call thee fickle; | 60 |

Lady Capulet greets her daughter and asks her how she is. She sympathises with Juliet's grief at the death of Tybalt and her hatred of the villain Romeo.

62–3   **Be fickle ... long** She wants fortune to be unreliable: just now fortune is taking Romeo away from her, but if it changes its mind then it will bring him back again.

67   **What ... hither?** What unusual reason brings her here?

71   **An if** Even if

72–3   **some grief ... wit** if you grieve a little it shows how much you loved (Tybalt); but if you grieve excessively it suggests that you are rather simple

75–6   **So shall ... weep for** If you do that you will experience the sense of loss but you won't bring back the friend you are grieving for

78–9   **thou weep'st ... him** you aren't really weeping because Tybalt is dead but because Romeo, his killer, is still alive

81   **Villain ... asunder** Romeo is very far from being a villain

83   **And yet ... heart** and yet no man saddens me as much as he does

85   **from ... hands** beyond my reach

86   **Would ... venge** I wish I were the only person to avenge

If thou art fickle, what dost thou with him
That is renowned for faith? Be fickle, fortune;
For then I hope thou wilt not keep him long,
But send him back.

[She goes down from the window

Enter LADY CAPULET

L. CAPULET	Ho daughter, are you up?
JULIET	Who is't that calls? It is my lady mother. 65
	Is she not down so late, or up so early?
	What unaccustomed cause procures her hither?
L. CAPULET	Why how now Juliet?
JULIET	Madam I am not well.
L. CAPULET	Evermore weeping for your cousin's death?
	What, wilt thou wash him from his grave with
	tears? 70
	An if thou couldst, thou couldst not make him live.
	Therefore have done; some grief shows much of
	love,
	But much of grief shows still some want of wit.
JULIET	Yet let me weep for such a feeling loss.
L. CAPULET	So shall you feel the loss, but not the friend 75
	Which you weep for.
JULIET	Feeling so the loss,
	I cannot choose but ever weep the friend.
L. CAPULET	Well girl, thou weep'st not so much for his death,
	As that the villain lives which slaughtered him.
JULIET	What villain madam?
L. CAPULET	That same villain Romeo. 80
JULIET	*[Aside]* Villain and he be many miles asunder –
	God pardon him; I do, with all my heart;
	And yet no man like he doth grieve my heart.
l. capulet	That is because the traitor murderer lives.
juliet	Ay madam, from the reach of these my hands. 85
	Would none but I might venge my cousin's death.

Juliet appears to agree with her mother's attack on Romeo, but uses words that can also mean that she loves Romeo. Lady Capulet then turns to the question of marriage and tells Juliet to prepare to be married to Paris in two days' time. Juliet is horrified and tells her mother that she will do no such thing.

89   **runagate** fugitive

90   **unaccustomed dram** unexpected dose (of poison)

93–5 **Indeed ... vexed** Juliet's mother takes her to mean 'I never shall be satisfied with Romeo till I behold him dead. My poor heart is so vexed for a kinsman (Tybalt).' What she actually means is 'I never shall be satisfied with Romeo till I behold him. My poor heart is so vexed for a kinsman (Romeo) that it is dead.'

97   **temper** She means 'water it down', but her mother thinks she means 'mix it up'.

98   **upon receipt thereof** when he gets it

99–100 O how ... him Again she speaks with a double meaning. She wants Romeo to be with her so that she can show him her love. Lady Capulet assumes she means that she wants to avenge herself on Romeo for Tybalt's death.

101   **wreak** express

107   **careful** thoughtful

108   **to put ... heaviness** to save you from your sadness

110   **nor I ... for** and I wasn't expecting either

112   **Marry** An expression of surprise, from 'Mary', the mother of Jesus.

L. CAPULET	We will have vengeance for it, fear thou not.
	Then weep no more. I'll send to one in Mantua,
	Where that same banished runagate doth live,
	Shall give him such an unaccustomed dram, 90
	That he shall soon keep Tybalt company
	And then I hope thou wilt be satisfied.
JULIET	Indeed I never shall be satisfied
	With Romeo, till I behold him – dead –
	Is my poor heart so for a kinsman vexed. 95
	Madam, if you could find out but a man
	To bear a poison, I would temper it,
	That Romeo should upon receipt thereof
	Soon sleep in quiet. O how my heart abhors
	To hear him named – and cannot come to him – 100
	To wreak the love I bore my cousin
	Upon his body that hath slaughtered him.
L. CAPULET	Find thou the means, and I'll find such a man.
	But now I'll tell thee joyful tidings girl.
JULIET	And joy comes well in such a needy time. 105
	What are they, I beseech your ladyship?
L. CAPULET	Well, well, thou hast a careful father child,
	One who to put thee from thy heaviness
	Hath sorted out a sudden day of joy,
	That thou expects not, nor I looked not for. 110
JULIET	Madam, in happy time what day is that?
L. CAPULET	Marry my child, early next Thursday morn,
	The gallant, young and noble gentleman,
	The County Paris, at Saint Peter's Church,
	Shall happily make thee there a joyful bride. 115
JULIET	Now by Saint Peter's Church, and Peter too,
	He shall not make me there a joyful bride.
	I wonder at this haste, that I must wed
	Ere he that should be husband comes to woo.
	I pray you tell my lord and father, madam, 120
	I will not marry yet, and when I do, I swear
	It shall be Romeo, whom you know I hate,

Juliet's father enters, unaware of what Juliet has just said to her mother, and comments on his daughter's grief. His wife tells him that Juliet has refused to marry Paris. Capulet is amazed to hear this and questions her about it. When she repeats her refusal Capulet loses his temper.

126 **When ... dew** The idea here is that dew is produced at the end of a sunny day because the sun is going away and the earth is sad, so it weeps a little (drizzle rather than rain).

129 **conduit** water pipe

131 **counterfeits** (short for 'counterfeitest') represent, imitate

133 **bark** boat

134–7 **the winds ... body** The winds in his comparison are Juliet's sighs which blow as she weeps and unless there is a sudden calm they will capsize the boat (her body) which is being thrown about by the storm.

138 **our decree** what I have decided (He uses 'our' as if he was a king.)

139 **she will none** she will have nothing to do with it

141 **take me with you** explain what you mean

144 **wrought** arranged

146–8 **Not ... love** I am not proud of what you have done, but grateful to you (for the thought it shows); I can never be proud of something I hate but I can be grateful for something hateful if it was offered with love

149 **chopt-logic** quibbling

151 **minion** hussy

153 **fettle ... 'gainst** prepare yourself for

155 **I will ... hurdle** Wongdoers were often dragged through the streets on a piece of fencing pulled behind a horse.

156 **green-sickness carrion** He is saying that she looks as anaemic as a corpse.

Rather than Paris. These are news indeed.

L. CAPULET   Here comes your father, tell him so yourself,
And see how he will take it at your hands.   125

Enter CAPULET *and* NURSE

CAPULET   When the sun sets, the earth doth drizzle dew;
But for the sunset of my brother's son
It rains downright.
How now, a conduit, girl? What, still in tears?
Evermore showering? In one little body   130
Thou counterfeits a bark, a sea, a wind.
For still thy eyes, which I may call the sea,
Do ebb and flow with tears; the bark thy body is
Sailing in this salt flood; the winds, thy sighs,
Who raging with thy tears, and they with them,   135
Without a sudden calm, will overset
Thy tempest-tossed body. How now wife,
Have you delivered to her our decree?

L. CAPULET   Ay sir, but she will none, she gives you thanks.
I would the fool were married to her grave.   140

CAPULET   Soft, take me with you, take me with you wife.
How will she none? Doth she not give us thanks?
Is she not proud? Doth she not count her blessed,
Unworthy as she is, that we have wrought
So worthy a gentleman to be her bride?   145

JULIET   Not proud you have, but thankful that you have.
Proud can I never be of what I hate,
But thankful even for hate, that is meant love.

CAPULET   How, how, how, how, chopt-logic? What is this?
'Proud', and 'I thank you', and 'I thank you not',   150
And yet 'not proud'. Mistress minion you,
Thank me no thankings, nor proud me no prouds,
But fettle your fine joints 'gainst Thursday next,
To go with Paris to Saint Peter's Church,
Or I will drag thee on a hurdle thither.   155
Out you green-sickness carrion, out you baggage,

Capulet tells Juliet that either she will marry Paris on Thursday or he will disown her. The Nurse tries to defend Juliet, only to be shouted down by Capulet, who complains bitterly of Juliet's ingratitude.

157   **tallow-face** white face

160   **baggage** hussy

161   **a** on

168   **hilding** worthless child

171   **Good prudence** Prudence may be the Nurse's name, but more likely Capulet is being sarcastic and telling her how 'thoughtful' and 'sensible' she is.

       smatter chatter

172   **God ye god-den** goodbye – he means 'Be off with you!'

174   **gravity** serious advice (He is being sarcastic.)

       gossip's bowl the drink she has while she is nattering to her friends

175   **hot** angry, hot-tempered

176   **God's bread** He swears by the sacrament of the bread in the Mass.

179   **matched** married

181   **demesnes** estates

       liened descended

182   **Stuffed ... parts** absolutely full of good qualities

184   **puling** weeping

185   **mammet** doll

       in ... tender when by chance she receives a good offer (of marriage)

	You tallow-face!	
L. CAPULET	Fie, fie, what, are you mad?	
JULIET	Good father, I beseech you on my knees,	
	[She kneels down	
	Hear me with patience, but to speak a word.	
CAPULET	Hang thee young baggage, disobedient wretch!	160
	I tell thee what, get thee to church a Thursday,	
	Or never after look me in the face.	
	Speak not, reply not, do not answer me.	
	My fingers itch. Wife, we scarce thought us blessed	
	That God had sent us but this only child;	165
	But now I see this one is one too much,	
	And that we have a curse in having her.	
	Out on her, hilding!	
NURSE	God in heaven bless her.	
	You are to blame my lord to rate her so.	
CAPULET	And why, my lady wisdom? Hold your tongue.	170
	Good prudence, smatter with your gossips, go.	
NURSE	I speak no treason.	
CAPULET	O God ye god-den.	
NURSE	May not one speak?	
CAPULET	Peace you mumbling fool.	
	Utter your gravity o'er a gossip's bowl,	
	For here we need it not.	
L. CAPULET	You are too hot.	175
CAPULET	God's bread, it makes me mad.	
	Day, night, hour, tide, time, work, play,	
	Alone, in company, still my care hath been	
	To have her matched; and having now provided	
	A gentleman of noble parentage,	180
	Of fair demesnes, youthful and nobly liened,	
	Stuffed as they say with honourable parts,	
	Proportioned as one's thought would wish a man –	
	And then to have a wretched puling fool,	
	A whining mammet, in her fortune's tender,	

Still in a towering rage at Juliet's rejection of all the loving attention she has received from her parents, Capulet storms off. Juliet speaks self-pityingly but receives no comfort from her mother who also leaves her. She turns to the Nurse for comfort in her predicament.

188   **and** if

189   **Graze** Feed (He uses the word normally used for cows and other animals.)

190   **I do ... jest** I am not accustomed to joking

191   **advise** think about it

192   **give** (He sees Juliet as a piece of property to be given away.)

194   **acknowledge** recognise you as my daughter

195   **Nor ... good** (He is threatening to disinherit her.)

196   **bethink you** think about it

      I'll not be forsworn I shall not change my mind

202   **that dim monument** the family vault

206–9   **My husband ... earth?** Juliet means that when she married Romeo she gave a promise to heaven to be faithful to him. Until he dies and goes to heaven her promise will not be returned to her from heaven, freeing her to marry again.

210   **practise stratagems** play tricks

214–15   **all the world ... you** I'll bet you anything he won't dare come back to question your actions

217   **Then ... doth** So as things stand

To answer 'I'll not wed, I cannot love,
I am too young, I pray you pardon me' –
But and you will not wed, I'll pardon you.
Graze where you will, you shall not house with me.
Look to't, think on't, I do not use to jest.   190
Thursday is near, lay hand on heart, advise.
And you be mine, I'll give you to my friend;
And you be not, hang, beg, starve, die in the streets,
For by my soul, I'll ne'er acknowledge thee,
Nor what is mine shall never do thee good.   195
Trust to't, bethink you, I'll not be forsworn.

                                               [*Exit*

JULIET   Is there no pity sitting in the clouds,
That sees into the bottom of my grief?
O sweet my mother cast me not away.
Delay this marriage for a month, a week,   200
Or if you do not, make the bridal bed
In that dim monument where Tybalt lies.

L. CAPULET   Talk not to me, for I'll not speak a word.
Do as thou wilt, for I have done with thee.

                                               [*Exit*

JULIET   O God! O Nurse, how shall this be prevented?   205
My husband is on earth, my faith in heaven;
How shall that faith return again to earth,
Unless that husband send it me from heaven
By leaving earth? Comfort me, counsel me.
Alack, alack, that heaven should practise
    stratagems   210
Upon so soft a subject as myself!
What sayest thou, hast thou not a word of joy?
Some comfort, Nurse.

NURSE   Faith here it is. Romeo
Is banished, and all the world to nothing,
That he dares ne'er come back to challenge you;   215
Or if he do, it needs must be by stealth.
Then since the case so stands as now it doth,

The Nurse advises Juliet to forget about Romeo and to marry Paris as her parents wish. Juliet asks her if that is what she really means and the Nurse says that it is. Juliet says that she accepts this advice; the Nurse is to tell her mother that she is sorry that she has upset her father and is going to see Friar Lawrence to make her confession. As soon as the Nurse has gone, Juliet expresses her true feelings about the Nurse's treachery. She will never confide in her again; instead she will go and ask Friar Lawrence's advice.

220	**dishclout**	dishcloth
221	**green, so ... quick**	lively and sharp
222	**Beshrew my very heart**	May my heart be cursed if I am wrong, but
224	**it excels**	it is even better than
226	**As living hence**	because he lives somewhere else
228	**Amen**	So be it, I agree
234	**Ancient damnation**	Wicked old woman
	fiend	devil
235	**forsworn**	having broken my word
236–7	**Or to ... compare**	or to criticise Romeo with the same tongue she used in the past to praise him to the skies
238	**counsellor**	adviser
239	**Thou ... twain**	I will never confide in you again

I think it best you married with the County.
O he's a lovely gentleman.
Romeo's a dishclout to him; an eagle, madam,   220
Hath not so green, so quick, so fair an eye
As Paris hath. Beshrew my very heart,
I think you are happy in this second match,
For it excels your first; or if it did not,
Your first is dead, or't were as good he were,   225
As living hence, and you no use of him.

JULIET   Speak'st thou from thy heart?

NURSE   And from my soul too.
Or else beshrew them both.

JULIET   Amen.

NURSE   What?

JULIET   Well thou hast comforted me marvellous much.
Go in, and tell my lady I am gone,   230
Having displeased my father, to Lawrence' cell,
To make confession, and to be absolved.

NURSE   Marry I will, and this is wisely done.

[*Exit*

She looks after NURSE

JULIET   Ancient damnation! O most wicked fiend!
Is it more sin to wish me thus forsworn,   235
Or to dispraise my lord with that same tongue
Which she hath praised him with above compare
So many thousand times? Go counsellor;
Thou and my bosom henceforth shall be twain.
I'll to the friar to know his remedy.   240
If all else fail, myself have power to die.

[*Exit*

Act 3 scene 5

Contrasts

Act 3 scene 5 contains a lot of contrasting action. The central character
is Juliet and we watch as she is buffeted this way and that by events she
cannot control. We can divide the scene into five main sections. Copy
the table and fill in the missing sections:

Lines	Title	Action
1–64	Romeo and Juliet part.	Juliet begs Romeo to stay. She argues that it is still night. Romeo agrees, knowing that it will mean his death. Juliet relents, they say their sad farewells, and Romeo leaves.
65–103	Lady Capulet brings news of the wedding.	
104–25		
126–96		
197–241		

Juliet's thoughts

Act 3 scene 5 is a real challenge for the actor playing the part of Juliet.
In rehearsal she has to work out how her thoughts and feelings shift
and change as the scene develops. The 12 notes opposite describe her
thoughts.

1   The notes are out of sequence. Put them in the right order.
2   Now find the point in the scene that each note refers to. Write
    down the line reference for each note.

She cannot believe what she is hearing from the Nurse – she's completely changed sides.

A

Her father's anger is worse than she has ever known. How can she stop him before he attacks her?

B

She has a terrible foreboding: she has a vision of Romeo lying dead in his tomb.

C

That's it. She's on her own. She will have to look after herself. Friar Lawrence is her only hope.

D

No, it really is getting light. Romeo must go now, before it is too late and he is captured.

E

There is only her dear Nurse left: perhaps she can advise her on what to do.

F

Now that her father's gone, perhaps she can beg her mother to help her.

G

She doesn't want Romeo to leave, and wishes the night could last forever.

H

She can't believe it! How can her mother possibly think she wants to marry Paris on Thursday?

I

What can she say about Tybalt, without letting on that she loves Romeo?

J

How is she going to face her father? He's terrifying when he's in one of his rages.

K

What on earth can her mother want at this time of the night? What is she to do?

L

The Capulet family

Act 3 scene 5 contains a huge family row which is triggered when Juliet refuses to marry Paris. Her father's anger is all the more shocking when you remember how he first spoke to Paris about marrying Juliet. To understand this you need to look back through the play to find the other occasions when Capulet has spoken about Juliet and her possible marriage.

Work with a partner

1   The four short speeches below are all spoken by Capulet. They are not in the correct order.

   a   Write them out in their correct order and number them.

   b   Against each one, write the scene in which it appears and the line numbers.

   i   *I think she will be ruled*
       In all respects by me; nay more, I doubt it not.

   ii   *Things have fall'n out sir, so unluckily,*
       That we have had no time to move our daughter.

   iii   *Thursday, tell her*
       She shall be married to this noble earl.

   iv   *But woo her gentle Paris, get her heart,*
       My will to her consent is but a part.

2   For each speech, write an explanation in your own words of what it tells us about Capulet's attitude towards his daughter and her marriage to Paris.

3   For speeches ii, iii, and iv, write a short explanation of how his attitude has changed since the previous speech.

4   Now talk about:

   a   why you think his attitude has changed in this way

   b   how and why it has changed again by the beginning of Act 3 scene 5.

Work in a group of four

5   Share your ideas. What do you think these scenes tell us about the whole of the Capulet family?

Performance: Capulet's speech

Lines 176–96 contain the climax of the family row. By this point, even Capulet's wife thinks he is out of control – 'You are too hot', she says. But it has no effect.

Work in a group of four

1   Begin by reading the speech silently on your own.

2   Now read it aloud, with each member of the group taking one line. Go round the group as many times as you need to complete the whole speech. Try to make it flow as smoothly as possible: you will need to concentrate so that you don't leave a gap when it is your turn to speak.

3   Now read it aloud again. But this time each read a whole section that ends with:

   • a full stop, or
   • a semi-colon, or
   • a dash.

   Before you begin, take a moment to work out where these breaks come.

4   Take a break to discuss how that reading went. Then try it again in exactly the same way. This time:

   • make it run as smoothly as you can
   • communicate as much of Capulet's rage as you can.

5   Practise your reading until you are satisfied that you are performing it as you planned.

6   Share it with the rest of the class.

Count Paris tells Friar Lawrence that Capulet has decided that his wedding to Juliet should be on Thursday. Although this is very soon after the funeral of Tybalt it will help to ease Juliet's grief. Juliet and Paris meet. Paris tries to persuade her to think of him as her future husband but Juliet rebuffs him.

2	**father** Capulet is about to become his father-in-law.
3	**I am ... haste** I have no reason to slow him down
4	**mind** feelings on the subject
5	**Uneven is the course** This way of proceeding is irregular
6	**Immoderately** Excessively
8	**For Venus smiles not** the Goddess of love is out of place
9–10	**counts ... sway** considers it bad for her to be so deep in grief
12	**inundation of her tears** her floods of tears
13–14	**too much ... society** she dwells too much on sorrow when she is on her own; companionship may help change her mood
16	**I would ... slowed** Friar Lawrence and the audience know why haste is not a good idea. He speaks only for the audience to hear (it is an **aside** – see Glossary p. 288).
22	**Come ... father** Paris assumes that Juliet has come to confess her sins to her priest before her wedding.

Act Four

Scene ❶

Friar Lawrence's cell
Enter FRIAR LAWRENCE *and* PARIS

F. LAWRENCE	On Thursday sir? The time is very short.
PARIS	My father Capulet will have it so,
	And I am nothing slow to slack his haste.
F. LAWRENCE	You say you do not know the lady's mind?
	Uneven is the course, I like it not.

5

PARIS   Immoderately she weeps for Tybalt's death,
          And therefore have I little talked of love,
          For Venus smiles not in a house of tears.
          Now sir, her father counts it dangerous
          That she do give her sorrow so much sway;   10
          And in his wisdom hastes our marriage,
          To stop the inundation of her tears;
          Which too much minded by herself alone,
          May be put from her by society.
          Now do you know the reason of this haste.   15

F. LAWRENCE   [*Aside*] I would I knew not why it should be slowed.
                Look sir, here comes the lady toward my cell.

Enter JULIET

PARIS   Happily met, my lady and my wife.
JULIET   That may be sir, when I may be a wife.
PARIS   That 'may be' must be, love, on Thursday next.   20
JULIET   What must be shall be.
F. LAWRENCE   That's a certain text.
PARIS   Come you to make confession to this father?
JULIET   To answer that, I should confess to you.
PARIS   Do not deny to him that you love me.

When Paris leaves, Juliet begs Friar Lawrence to help her. If he cannot she is determined to kill herself rather than be married to Paris.

25	**I will ... him** Juliet now snubs Paris without allowing him to think his love is pointless. She continues to spar with him.
29	**abused with tears** spoilt because you have been crying
30–1	**The tears ... spite** the tears didn't achieve much then, my face was bad enough before they tried to spoil it
32	**Thou wrong'st it** You are being unkind (to your face)
39	**pensive** sad
40	**entreat** beg for
41	**God shield** God forbid
45	**past cure** there is nothing to be done, no way out
47	**past ... wits** beyond my grasp
48	**prorogue** postpone
49	**County** count
53	**resolution** decision
54	**presently** straight away
56–7	**And ere ... deed** In the wedding ceremony her hand and Romeo's were joined together to symbolise their marriage, as the seal on a document shows it is genuine. Juliet does not want her hand to be the seal ('label') for a second marriage contract.

| JULIET | I will confess to you that I love him. | 25 |

| PARIS | So will ye, I am sure, that you love me. | |

| JULIET | If I do so, it will be of more price, | |
| | Being spoke behind your back, than to your face. | |

| PARIS | Poor soul, thy face is much abused with tears. | |

| JULIET | The tears have got small victory by that, | 30 |
| | For it was bad enough before their spite. | |

| PARIS | Thou wrong'st it more than tears with that report. | |

| JULIET | That is no slander sir, which is a truth, | |
| | And what I spake, I spake it to my face. | |

| PARIS | Thy face is mine, and thou hast slandered it. | 35 |

JULIET	It may be so, for it is not mine own.	
	Are you at leisure holy father now,	
	Or shall I come to you at evening mass?	

| F. LAWRENCE | My leisure serves me pensive daughter now. | |
| | My lord, we must entreat the time alone. | 40 |

PARIS	God shield I should disturb devotion.	
	Juliet, on Thursday early will I rouse ye.	
	Till then adieu, and keep this holy kiss.	

[Exit

| JULIET | O shut the door, and when thou hast done so, | |
| | Come weep with me, past hope, past cure, past help. | 45 |

F. LAWRENCE	O Juliet I already know thy grief,	
	It strains me past the compass of my wits.	
	I hear thou must, and nothing may prorogue it,	
	On Thursday next be married to this County.	

JULIET	Tell me not Friar, that thou hearest of this,	50
	Unless thou tell me how I may prevent it.	
	If in thy wisdom thou canst give no help,	
	Do thou but call my resolution wise,	
	And with this knife I'll help it presently.	
	God joined my heart and Romeo's, thou our hands;	55
	And ere this hand, by thee to Romeo's sealed,	
	Shall be the label to another deed,	
	Or my true heart with treacherous revolt	

The Friar says that if she is prepared to face death, then he has a remedy that may work. He tells her to pretend to agree to the marriage. Then, the night before the wedding, she must take the potion he gives her.

62   **extremes** desperate situation

63–5   **arbitrating ... bring** sorting out the problem which all your experience could not honourably solve

67   **If what ... remedy** if what you say does not offer a solution

69–70 **Which ... prevent** which demands an action as extreme and ruthless as we are trying to prevent

73–5   **Then is it ... from it** then you, who are prepared to face death itself to escape from the shame of marrying Paris, are likely to be prepared to suffer something like death in order to avoid it

81   **charnel-house** A small building near a church where human bones were stored. When the bodies of the dead had been buried for some years, the graves were sometimes dug up and the bones placed in the charnel-house.

83   **reeky shanks** shinbones full of rank-smelling moisture

        chapless without a lower jaw

88   **unstained** pure

93   **vial** small bottle or flask

94   **distilling liquor** liquid that will penetrate the body

Turn to another, this shall slay them both.   60
Therefore out of thy long-experienced time,
Give me some present counsel, or behold
'Twixt my extremes and me this bloody knife
Shall play the umpire, arbitrating that
Which the commission of thy years and art   65
Could to no issue of true honour bring.
Be not so long to speak; I long to die,
If what thou speak'st speak not of remedy.

F. LAWRENCE   Hold daughter, I do spy a kind of hope,
Which craves as desperate an execution,   70
As that is desperate which we would prevent.
If, rather than to marry County Paris,
Thou hast the strength of will to slay thyself,
Then is it likely thou wilt undertake
A thing like death to chide away this shame,   75
That cop'st with death himself to 'scape from it;
And if thou darest, I'll give thee remedy.

JULIET   O bid me leap, rather than marry Paris,
From off the battlements of any tower;
Or walk in thievish ways; or bid me lurk
Where serpents are; chain me with roaring   80
    bears;
Or hide me nightly in a charnel-house,
O'er-covered quite with dead men's rattling bones,
With reeky shanks and yellow chapless skulls;
Or bid me go into a new-made grave,   85
And hide me with a dead man in his shroud;
– Things that to hear them told have made me
    tremble –
And I will do it without fear or doubt,
To live an unstained wife to my sweet love.

F. LAWRENCE   Hold then, go home, be merry, give consent   90
To marry Paris. Wednesday is tomorrow;
Tomorrow night look that thou lie alone,
Let not the Nurse lie with thee in thy chamber.
Take thou this vial, being then in bed,

The potion will send her to sleep and make it look as if she is dead. She will be taken to the family vault where she will eventually wake up. Meanwhile the Friar will alert Romeo who will come to her there and take her to Mantua. Juliet agrees to this plan and hurries home with the drug.

96	**humour** body fluid
97	**keep ... progress** beat in the normal way
	surcease stop
98	**testify** show that
100	**wanned** pale
	eyes' windows eyelids
102	**supple government** mobility
110	**In thy ... bier** the body dressed in her finest clothes carried in an open coffin
111	**borne** carried
113–14	**In the ... drift** Meanwhile Romeo will know what we have done by letter, in preparation for the moment when you wake up again
119	**toy** silly idea
120	**Abate ... it** reduce your courage to carry it out
122	**prosperous** successful
125	**strength ... afford** and strength give me the help I need

And this distilling liquor drink thou off;   95
When presently through all thy veins shall run
A cold and drowsy humour; for no pulse
Shall keep his native progress, but surcease;
No warmth, no breath, shall testify thou livest;
The roses in thy lips and cheeks shall fade   100
To wanned ashes; thy eyes' windows fall,
Like death when he shuts up the day of life.
Each part deprived of supple government,
Shall stiff and stark and cold appear like death,
And in this borrowed likeness of shrunk death   105
Thou shalt continue two and forty hours,
And then awake as from a pleasant sleep.
Now when the bridegroom in the morning comes
To rouse thee from thy bed, there art thou dead.
Then as the manner of our country is,   110
In thy best robes uncovered on the bier,
Thou shalt be borne to that same ancient vault,
Where all the kindred of the Capulets lie.
In the mean time, against thou shalt awake,
Shall Romeo by my letters know our drift,   115
And hither shall he come; and he and I
Will watch thy waking, and that very night
Shall Romeo bear thee hence to Mantua.
And this shall free thee from this present shame,
If no inconstant toy nor womanish fear   120
Abate thy valour in the acting it.

JULIET   Give me, give me. O tell not me of fear.

F. LAWRENCE   Hold. Get you gone, be strong and prosperous
                In this resolve. I'll send a friar with speed
                To Mantua, with my letters to thy lord.

JULIET   Love give me strength, and strength shall help   125
                    afford.
                Farewell dear father.

                                              [*Exeunt*

Capulet is busying himself making preparations for the wedding: sending out invitations and hiring cooks. Juliet returns from her visit to Friar Lawrence and immediately asks her father to forgive her for her earlier behaviour.

1   **So many ... writ** Capulet hands a list of guests to a servant who is to invite them.

2   **cunning** skilful

3   **none ill** no bad ones

       try test, see

4   **lick their fingers** They are good cooks if they enjoy tasting what they are cooking.

10   **unfurnished** ill-prepared

12   **Ay forsooth** Yes, indeed

14   **A peevish ... it is** she is a headstrong and obstinate silly girl

15   **shrift** confession

16   **headstrong** self-willed girl

       gadding wandering off to

19   **behests** instructions, commands

       enjoined made to promise

20   **prostrate** face down on the ground (to humble herself before her father)

24   **knot knit up** business tied up

26   **becomed** suitable, proper

Scene ❷

Capulet's mansion
Enter CAPULET, LADY CAPULET, NURSE, *and* SERVANTS

CAPULET	So many guests invite as here are writ.

                              [Exit First Servant

	Sirrah, go hire me twenty cunning cooks.	
2ND SERVANT	You shall have none ill sir, for I'll try if they can lick their fingers.	
CAPULET	How canst thou try them so?	5
2ND SERVANT	Marry sir, 'tis an ill cook that cannot lick his own fingers; therefore he that cannot lick his own fingers goes not with me.	
CAPULET	Go, be gone. *[Exit*	
	We shall be much unfurnished for this time.	10
	What, is my daughter gone to Friar Lawrence?	
NURSE	Ay forsooth.	
CAPULET	Well, he may chance to do some good on her; A peevish self-willed harlotry it is.	
NURSE	See where she comes from shrift with merry look.	15

Enter JULIET

CAPULET	How now my headstrong, where have you been gadding?	
JULIET	Where I have learned me to repent the sin Of disobedient opposition To you and your behests, and am enjoined By holy Lawrence to fall prostrate here, To beg your pardon. Pardon I beseech you, Henceforward I am ever ruled by you.	20
CAPULET	Send for the County, go tell him of this. I'll have this knot knit up tomorrow morning.	
JULIET	I met the youthful lord at Lawrence' cell, And gave him what becomed love I might, Not stepping o'er the bounds of modesty.	25

Capulet is delighted and decides that the wedding shall be a day earlier, on the Wednesday rather than the Thursday. Juliet and the Nurse go off to prepare for the wedding.

34	**ornaments** clothes	
36	**Thursday** Lady Capulet still thinks that the wedding should be on the Thursday.	
37	**tomorrow** Her husband overrules her.	
38	**We ... provision** We shan't be ready in time	
40	**warrant** promise, guarantee	
43–4	**What ho! ... forth** He calls for one of the servants and then remembers he has sent them all off on errands.	
47	**Since ... reclaimed** since this self-willed girl has changed her ways	

Juliet asks the Nurse to leave her as she wishes to spend the night on her own.

1	**attires** clothes
3	**orisons** prayers
5	**cross** perverse

CAPULET	Why I am glad on't; this is well. Stand up.
	This is as 't should be. Let me see the County.
	Ay marry go, I say, and fetch him hither. 30
	Now afore God, this reverend holy friar,
	All our whole city is much bound to him.
JULIET	Nurse, will you go with me into my closet,
	To help me sort such needful ornaments
	As you think fit to furnish me tomorrow? 35
L. CAPULET	No, not till Thursday, there is time enough.
CAPULET	Go Nurse, go with her; we'll to church tomorrow.

[*Exeunt* JULIET *and* NURSE

L. CAPULET	We shall be short in our provision;
	'Tis now near night.
CAPULET	Tush, I will stir about,
	And all things shall be well, I warrant thee wife. 40
	Go thou to Juliet, help to deck up her;
	I'll not to bed tonight, let me alone.
	I'll play the housewife for this once. What ho!
	They are all forth. Well, I will walk myself
	To County Paris, to prepare up him 45
	Against tomorrow. My heart is wondrous light,
	Since this same wayward girl is so reclaimed.

[*Exeunt*

Scene ❸

Juliet's bedroom
Enter JULIET *and* NURSE

JULIET	Ay, those attires are best; but gentle Nurse,
	I pray thee leave me to myself tonight;
	For I have need of many orisons,
	To move the heavens to smile upon my state,
	Which well thou knowest is cross and full of sin. 5

Juliet says goodnight to her mother and then is left alone. She takes out the drug which the Friar has given her and immediately begins to have doubts perhaps it won't work; perhaps it is really a poison because the Friar wants her dead to save his reputation.

7–8	**culled ... tomorrow** collected together all the things we need for tomorrow
19	**My dismal ... alone** I've got to do this sad deed on my own
20	**vial** the small bottle containing the drug that Friar Lawrence has given her
25	**Subtly hath ministered** has secretly given me
26	**Lest** in case
29	**tried** proved by experience to be
32	**redeem** rescue
37	**The horrible ... night** Juliet is thinking of the effects that darkness and the nearness of so many dead bodies will have on her imagination ('conceit').

Enter LADY CAPULET

L. CAPULET	What, are you busy, ho? Need you my help?
JULIET	No madam, we have culled such necessaries

As are behoveful for our state tomorrow.
So please you, let me now be left alone,
And let the Nurse this night sit up with you;   10
For I am sure you have your hands full all,
In this so sudden business.

L. CAPULET   Good night.
Get thee to bed and rest, for thou hast need.

                    [*Exeunt* LADY CAPULET *and* NURSE

JULIET   Farewell. God knows when we shall meet again.
I have a faint cold fear thrills through my veins,   15
That almost freezes up the heat of life.
I'll call them back again to comfort me.
Nurse! What should she do here?
My dismal scene I needs must act alone.
Come vial.   20
What if this mixture do not work at all?
Shall I be married then tomorrow morning?
No, no, this shall forbid it. Lie thou there.

                              [*Lays down a dagger*

What if it be a poison which the friar
Subtly hath ministered to have me dead,   25
Lest in this marriage he should be dishonoured,
Because he married me before to Romeo?
I fear it is, and yet methinks it should not,
For he hath still been tried a holy man.
How if when I am laid into the tomb,   30
I wake before the time that Romeo
Come to redeem me? There's a fearful point.
Shall I not then be stifled in the vault,
To whose foul mouth no healthsome air breathes in,
And there die strangled ere my Romeo comes?   35
Or if I live, is it not very like,
The horrible conceit of death and night,

She puts these thoughts to one side, only to be assailed by other fears of suffocation in the tomb and of going mad with fear when she wakes up. At last Juliet overcomes her doubts and swallows the liquid.

42   **yet ... earth** only recently buried

44   **resort** meet up

47   **mandrake** A plant with a forked root that, because it resembled the shape of a human body, was believed to shriek when pulled out of the ground.

49   **distraught** driven mad

50   **Environed with** surrounded by

52   **mangled** cut about

56   **spit** skewer

In the Capulets' house everyone is busy making last-minute preparations for the wedding.

1   **Hold** Here

2   **quinces** hard yellowish pear-shaped fruit with a distinctive flavour

     the pastry a room (presumably kept cold) where pastry was made

3   **stir, stir, stir** hurry, hurry, hurry

     the second ... crowed The first cock crow was held to be at midnight, the second at 3 a.m.

4   **curfew bell** Originally a bell rung in the evening to remind people to put out domestic fires (from the French *couvre-feu*).

5   **Look ... meats** Check the meat pies

     Angelica A Christian name for one of the servants, or possibly the Nurse.

Together with the terror of the place –
As in a vault, an ancient receptacle,
Where for this many hundred years the bones   40
Of all my buried ancestors are packed,
Where bloody Tybalt yet but green in earth
Lies festering in his shroud, where as they say,
At some hours in the night spirits resort –
Alack, alack, is it not like that I,   45
So early waking – what with loathsome smells,
And shrieks like mandrakes' torn out of the earth,
That living mortals hearing them, run mad –
O if I wake, shall I not be distraught,
Environed with all these hideous fears,   50
And madly play with my forefathers' joints,
And pluck the mangled Tybalt from his shroud,
And in this rage, with some great kinsman's bone,
As with a club, dash out my desperate brains?
O look, methinks I see my cousin's ghost   55
Seeking out Romeo that did spit his body
Upon a rapier's point – stay Tybalt, stay!
Romeo! Romeo! Romeo! I drink to thee.

       [She falls upon her bed within the curtains

Scene ④

A room in Capulet's mansion
Enter LADY CAPULET *and* NURSE *with herbs*

L. CAPULET   Hold, take these keys, and fetch more spices,
           Nurse.

NURSE   They call for dates and quinces in the pastry.

      Enter CAPULET

CAPULET   Come, stir, stir, stir, the second cock hath crowed,
           The curfew bell hath rung, 'tis three o'clock.
           Look to the baked meats, good Angelica.   5

Capulet is rushing around getting in everyone's way and thoroughly enjoying himself.

6	**Spare ... cost** The expense is not important
	cot-quean a man who takes a housewife's duties on himself
7	**sick** ill
8	**watching** staying up all night
9	**not a whit** not at all
	ere now before now
11	**a mouse-hunt** Literally, an animal that hunts for mice, usually at night. But at this time 'mouse' also meant 'sweetheart', so she means 'woman hunter'.
12	**But ... watching** I will keep an eye on such things now
13	**A jealous hood** A jealous woman
SD	*spits* Heavy metal skewers on which meat would be roasted at an open fire.
18–19	**I have ... matter** The servant, joking, suggests that his wooden head will easily lead him to logs.
20	**Mass** Capulet exclaims by swearing 'by the mass', a church service.
	merry whoreson cheerful fellow
21	**logger-head** 1) the chief fetcher of logs 2) a blockhead
22	**straight** straight away
25	**go ... up** go and get her ready
26	**Hie, make haste** Hurry up, be quick

Spare not for cost.

NURSE   Go you cot-quean, go,
Get you to bed; faith you'll be sick tomorrow
For this night's watching.

CAPULET   No, not a whit; what, I have watched ere now
All night for lesser cause, and ne'er been sick.   10

L. CAPULET   Ay you have been a mouse-hunt in your time,
But I will watch you from such watching now.

[*Exeunt* LADY CAPULET *and* NURSE

CAPULET   A jealous hood, a jealous hood.

Enter three or four SERVING-MEN, *with spits, and
logs, and baskets*

                                  Now fellow,
What is there?

SERVING-MAN   Things for the cook sir, but I know not what.   15

CAPULET   Make haste, make haste. Sirrah fetch drier logs.
Call Peter, he will show thee where they are.

SERVING-MAN   I have a head sir, that will find out logs,
And never trouble Peter for the matter.

[*Exit*

CAPULET   Mass and well said, a merry whoreson, ha!   20
Thou shalt be logger-head. Good faith, 'tis day.
The County will be here with music straight,
For so he said he would. I hear him near.

[*Music within*

Nurse! Wife! What ho! What, Nurse I say!

Enter NURSE

Go waken Juliet, go and trim her up.   25
I'll go and chat with Paris. Hie, make haste,
Make haste; the bridegroom he is come already.
Make haste I say.

[*Exeunt*

The Nurse goes to wake Juliet. At first she thinks she is very soundly asleep but gradually she realises that she is dead. Lady Capulet and her husband enter the bedroom and are horrified at this news.

1   **Fast** (asleep)

     I warrant her I'll bet

2   **slug-a-bed** sluggard, lazybones

4   **take your pennyworths** get what little bits of sleep you can now

6–7 **hath ... little** has put all his money (as in a game of cards) on it that you won't get much sleep tomorrow night

15   **weraday** alas

16   **aqua vitae** brandy

Scene ⑤

Juliet's bedroom

NURSE	Mistress! What, mistress! Juliet! Fast, I warrant
	her. She –
	Why lamb, why lady – fie you slug-a-bed!
	Why love I say! Madam! Sweetheart! Why bride!
	What, not a word? You take your pennyworths now.
	Sleep for a week; for the next night I warrant 5
	The County Paris hath set up his rest
	That you shall rest but little. God forgive me.
	Marry, and amen. How sound is she asleep!
	I needs must wake her. Madam, madam, madam!
	Ay, let the County take you in your bed, 10
	He'll fright you up i' faith. Will it not be?

                      [Draws back the curtains

	What, dressed, and in your clothes, and down again?
	I must needs wake you. Lady, lady, lady!
	Alas, alas, help, help, my lady's dead!
	O weraday that ever I was born! 15
	Some aqua vitae ho! My lord! My lady!

Enter LADY CAPULET

L. CAPULET	What noise is here?
NURSE	O lamentable day!
L. CAPULET	What is the matter?
NURSE	Look, look. O heavy day!
L. CAPULET	O me, O me, my child, my only life.
	Revive, look up, or I will die with thee. 20
	Help, help! Call help.

Enter CAPULET

CAPULET	For shame, bring Juliet forth; her lord is come.
NURSE	She's dead, deceased, she's dead, alack the day!

The Friar and Paris also arrive and are equally distressed. All five grieve the sudden and shattering death of Juliet. Friar Lawrence tries to calm their grief.

26   **her blood is settled** her heart has stopped beating

31   **ta'en her hence** taken her away

37   **deflowered by him** lost her virginity to him

38–40 **Death is ... death's** Capulet sees death as a person who has married his daughter and will inherit all his goods – an example of **personification** (see Glossary p. 291).

45   **In lasting ... pilgrimage** through all the hard work of his journey

47   **solace** take comfort

48   **catched** snatched

55   **Beguiled** tricked

L. CAPULET	Alack the day, she's dead, she's dead, she's dead!
CAPULET	Ha! Let me see her. Out alas she's cold, 25
	Her blood is settled, and her joints are stiff;
	Life and these lips have long been separated.
	Death lies on her like an untimely frost
	Upon the sweetest flower of all the field.
NURSE	O lamentable day!
L. CAPULET	O woeful time! 30
CAPULET	Death that hath ta'en her hence to make me wail,
	Ties up my tongue, and will not let me speak.

Enter FRIAR LAWRENCE, PARIS, *and* MUSICIANS

F. LAWRENCE	Come, is the bride ready to go to church?
CAPULET	Ready to go, but never to return.
	O son, the night before thy wedding-day 35
	Hath death lain with thy wife; there she lies,
	Flower as she was, deflowered by him.
	Death is my son-in-law, death is my heir,
	My daughter he hath wedded. I will die,
	And leave him all; life, living, all is death's. 40
PARIS	Have I thought long to see this morning's face,
	And doth it give me such a sight as this?
L. CAPULET	Accursed, unhappy, wretched, hateful day,
	Most miserable hour that e'er time saw
	In lasting labour of his pilgrimage! 45
	But one, poor one, one poor and loving child,
	But one thing to rejoice and solace in,
	And cruel death hath catched it from my sight.
NURSE	O woe! O woeful, woeful, woeful day!
	Most lamentable day, most woeful day, 50
	That ever, ever, I did yet behold!
	O day! O day! O day! O hateful day!
	Never was seen so black a day as this.
	O woeful day! O woeful day!
PARIS	Beguiled, divorced, wronged, spited, slain, 55

Friar Lawrence tells them to remember that human beings are born to die and go to heaven, so they should be happy that Juliet is now in heaven. Capulet accepts his words and says that the wedding they had planned will now be transformed into a funeral.

60   **Uncomfortable** refusing to give us comfort

61   **solemnity** celebration

65   **Confusion** disaster

66–8   **Heaven ... maid** You only shared your daughter with Heaven

71   **her promotion** that she should do well

72   **be advanced** get on in life

75–6   **O in this ... well** In this way of showing your love, you actually love her so badly that it drives you mad to see she is dead

77–8   **She's not ... young** The woman who is married for a long time does not have a good marriage; the woman who dies young has the best marriage (The Friar is taking rather an extreme religious view if a woman dies young she has less chance to sin and goes to heaven. The Friar knows that Juliet isn't really dead and this might account for his 'callousness', but then we know from the Prologue that Juliet will die young.)

79–80 **stick ... corse** Rosemary, the herb that stood for remembrance, was used both at weddings and at funerals.

80   **corse** corpse

83   **Yet ... merriment** but common sense (which knows better) laughs at the tears which human nature makes us shed – because Juliet is in heaven

84–5   **All things ... funeral** Everything that we ordered to celebrate the wedding must now be transformed into what we need to mark a funeral

86   **melancholy** sad, gloomy

88   **solemn hymns** hymns to celebrate the wedding

           sullen dirges gloomy music (for the funeral)

90   **contrary** opposite

Most detestable death, by thee beguiled,
By cruel, cruel thee quite overthrown.
O love! O life! Not life, but love in death.

CAPULET Despised, distressed, hated, martyred, killed;
Uncomfortable time, why cam'st thou now   60
To murder, murder our solemnity?
O child! O child! My soul and not my child.
Dead art thou, alack my child is dead,
And with my child my joys are buried.

F. LAWRENCE Peace ho, for shame! Confusion's cure lives not   65
In these confusions. Heaven and yourself
Had part in this fair maid, now heaven hath all,
And all the better is it for the maid.
Your part in her you could not keep from death,
But heaven keeps his part in eternal life.   70
The most you sought was her promotion,
For 'twas your heaven she should be advanced;
And weep ye now, seeing she is advanced
Above the clouds, as high as heaven itself?
O in this love you love your child so ill,   75
That you run mad, seeing that she is well.
She's not well married that lives married long,
But she's best married that dies married young.
Dry up your tears, and stick your rosemary
On this fair corse; and as the custom is,   80
In all her best array bear her to church.
For though fond nature bids us all lament,
Yet nature's tears are reason's merriment.

CAPULET All things that we ordained festival
Turn from their office to black funeral   85
Our instruments to melancholy bells;
Our wedding cheer to a sad burial feast;
Our solemn hymns to sullen dirges change;
Our bridal flowers serve for a buried corse;
And all things change them to the contrary.   90

F. LAWRENCE Sir, go you in, and madam, go with him;

They all leave, except for the Nurse, who begins to prepare Juliet's body for burial. The musicians, who had been hired for the wedding, now arrive. Peter, the Nurse's servant, asks them to play, to cheer him up. They refuse and after some talk, they leave.

93   **corse** corpse

94   **lour** glower

SD   ***casting rosemary on her*** Rosemary is a sweet-smelling herb which was associated both with weddings and funerals.

96   **put ... gone** pack up our instruments and leave

99   **Ay ... amended** In the previous line the Nurse says the state of affairs ('case') is pitiful – the musician admits it could be better, but he may be referring to his instrument case.

101   **O and you ... 'Heart's ease'** If you want to keep me alive, play the song 'Heart's ease' (Peter is the one servant who has remained behind and he asks the musicians to play a song to 'ease' the distress he is in.)

104   **merry dump** Dump is a mournful song – it can't be 'merry'.

109   **I will ... soundly** All right I'll give you a sound beating then (with a musical **pun** on 'soundly')

111   **No money ... gleek** I won't give you money, I'll mock you

111–12 **give ... minstrel** call you a useless beggar

113–21 **Then will I give ... iron dagger** Peter and the musicians continue to fool about, making empty threats and **puns** on musical terms.

115   **pate** head

    carry no crotchets not put up with any nonsense

115–16 **I'll *re* you, I'll *fa* you** I'll beat you up (**puns** on re and fa, musical notes)

117   **An you ... note us** If you re and fa us, you'll take note of us

120–1 **Then ... dagger** Here comes the attack by my reason. I'll give you a good beating with an iron reason, and sheathe my metal dagger.

And go Sir Paris; every one prepare
To follow this fair corse unto her grave.
The heavens do lour upon you for some ill;
Move them no more by crossing their high will.   95

[*They all but the* NURSE *and* MUSICIANS *go forth, casting
rosemary on her and shutting the curtains*

1ST MUSICIAN	Faith we may put up our pipes and be gone.
NURSE	Honest good fellows, ah put up, put up, For well you know this is a pitiful case. [*Exit*
1ST MUSICIAN	Ay by my troth, the case may be amended.

Enter PETER

PETER	Musicians, O musicians, 'Heart's ease', 'Heart's ease'. 100 O and you will have me live, play 'Heart's ease'.
1ST MUSICIAN	Why 'Heart's ease'?
PETER	O musicians, because my heart itself plays 'My heart is full'. O play me some merry dump to comfort me. 105
1ST MUSICIAN	Not a dump, we, 'tis no time to play now.
PETER	You will not then?
1ST MUSICIAN	No.
PETER	I will then give it you soundly.
1ST MUSICIAN	What will you give us? 110
PETER	No money on my faith, but the gleek. I will give you the minstrel.
1ST MUSICIAN	Then will I give you the serving-creature.
PETER	Then will I lay the serving-creature's dagger on your pate. I will carry no crotchets. I'll *re* you, I'll 115 *fa* you. Do you note me?
1ST MUSICIAN	And you *re* us and *fa* us, you note us.
2ND MUSICIAN	Pray you put up your dagger, and put out your wit.
PETER	Then have at you with my wit. I will dry-beat 120 you with an iron wit, and put up my iron dagger.

Peter sets the musicians a riddle.

122–6 **Answer ... sound** Peter quotes a verse of song at the musicians, leaving out the last two lines. He then asks them by name why music should have a 'silver sound'.

127 **Catling** a string made from catgut (The musicians' names are all taken from musical instruments.)

129 **Rebeck** a three-stringed fiddle

132 **Soundpost** an essential part of a violin

138–9 **'Then ... redress'** Peter finishes his riddle.

doth lend redress puts things right

140 **pestilent knave** troublesome fellow, pest

141–2 **tarry ... dinner** hang around until the mourners come back and wait for dinner

Answer me like men.
>'When griping grief the heart doth wound,
>And doleful dumps the mind oppress,
>Then music with her silver sound' –   125

Why 'silver sound'? Why 'music with her silver sound'? What say you Simon Catling?

1st MUSICIAN   Marry sir, because silver hath a sweet sound.

PETER   Prates. What say you Hugh Rebeck?

2nd MUSICIAN   I say 'silver sound', because musicians sound for   130
silver.

PETER   Prates too. What say you James Soundpost?

3rd MUSICIAN   Faith I know not what to say.

PETER   O I cry you mercy; you are the singer. I will say
for you. It is 'music with her silver sound',   135
because such fellows as you have no gold for
sounding.
>'Then music with her silver sound,
>With speedy help doth lend redress.'

                                     [Exit

1st MUSICIAN   What a pestilent knave is this same!   140

2nd MUSICIAN   Hang him, Jack! Come we'll in here, tarry
for the mourners, and stay dinner.

                                  [Exeunt

Act 4 scenes 1 to 5

Juliet's character

What does Act 4 scene 1 reveal about Juliet?

Work with a partner

1 Use a table like the one below to explore what we might learn about Juliet at these points in the scene.

Line 59:   '...this shall slay them both.'

Lines 66–7:   'Be not so long ... speak not of remedy.'

Line 88:   '...live an unstained wife to my sweet love.'

Line 121:   'Give me, give me. O tell not me of fear.'

Words from text	What they might show	Explanation
'O shut the door... past help' (lines 44–5)	We might think Juliet is being over-dramatic and self-pitying, but she might just be genuinely pessimistic and desperate.	Repeating the word 'past' three times makes her words sound like a rehearsed speech: is she really in control of her emotions?

2 Here are two very different ways of describing Juliet in this scene:

   a clever with words

   b desperate.

   Decide on at least five other words or phrases that sum up Juliet at different points in this scene. Write the words down and give evidence to support each one.

3 Prepare a short presentation about what this scene tells us about Juliet's character.

Juliet's fears

Work on your own

1   Look carefully at Juliet's **soliloquy** in lines 14–58 of Act 4 scene 3.

2   The main part of this speech is devoted to Juliet's vision of what might go wrong after she has taken the Friar's drug. She imagines five different scenarios. Four of them are introduced by a phrase containing the word 'if'. The other begins with the words 'is it not like that ...'

3   Copy out this table:

Lines	Words	What Juliet is afraid of
	What if...	
	What if...	
	How if...	
	What if...	
	...is it not like that...	

4   Find the five scenarios and write down the line numbers for each.

5   In the column headed 'What Juliet is afraid of' write a description of her fears, using your own words.

6   Now read the speech again. Pick out two images that you find particularly vivid or striking. Write them down. For each one describe in your own words the picture they conjure up in your mind.

Work in a small group

7   Share your ideas in the group. Discuss this question: 'Which of Juliet's fears would you find most worrying and why?'

   a   Decide which of her fears you find most worrying.

   b   Make a list of the reasons for your choice.

   c   Decide how to present these ideas to the rest of the class.

8   Prepare a presentation on this for the rest of the class.

Staging solutions

The action of Act 4 scenes 4 and 5 is continuous. There isn't any break in time between when Capulet tells his wife and the Nurse to go and wake Juliet (scene 4 line 25) and when they enter her bedroom (scene 5 line 1). The director of a production has to think carefully about how to do this. The answer depends on the kind of staging.

Shakespearean staging

If necessary, refresh your memory by going back to pages 8–11. A plan of this kind of stage looks like this:

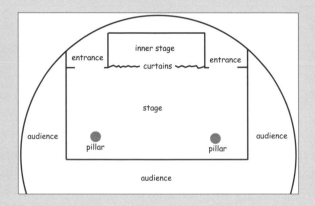

Work in a group of four

1   Discuss how you would direct these two scenes on this type of stage. In particular:

   a   where do you place Juliet's bedroom?

   b   how does the action move to this from the Capulets' mansion?

   c   how does it then move back out again?

2   Draw diagrams to show the position of the main characters at each of these seven points:

   •   Act 4 scene 4: lines 1, 14 and 25

   •   Act 4 scene 5: lines 1, 22 33, and 96.

Plot summary quiz

The 12 short quotations below sum up the story of Act 4.

1 Work out the correct order for them.

2 Work out who said each of them.

A

All things that we ordained festival Turn from their office to black funeral.

B

God forgive me. Marry, and amen. How sound is she asleep!

C

I have a faint cold fear thrills through my veins, That almost freezes up the heat of life.

D

Henceforward I am ever ruled by you.

E

My heart is wonderous light, Since this same wayward girl is so reclaimed.

F

Death lies upon her like an untimely frost Upon the sweetest flower of all the field.

G

Get you to bed; faith you'll be sick tomorrow For this night's watching.

H

Marry sir, 'tis an ill cook that cannot lick his own fingers.

I

Come weep with me, past hope, past cure, past help.

J

Uneven is the course, I like it not.

K

Love give me strength, and strength shall help afford.

L

Poor soul, thy face is much abused with tears.

In Mantua Romeo has dreamed that he was dead and that Juliet has brought him back to life with a kiss. Balthasar arrives from Verona with the news of Juliet's death. Romeo tells him to prepare for him to send a letter.

1	**the flattering ... sleep** when we sleep we sometimes have dreams which we believe because we want to believe them (since they flatter us)
2	**presage** foretell
3	**bosom's lord** heart
7	**leave** permission
10–11	**how ... joy** when dreams about love can make me so happy, how sweet my real love must be
18	**Capels' monument** the Capulets' tomb
19	**her immortal part** her soul
23	**did ... office** gave me that job to do
24	**I defy you, stars** The stars (which in astrology determine our futures) have ordained that Juliet shall die and so be taken away from Romeo. He is determined not to give in to this.
26	**post-horses** horses used to carry mail rapidly from one place to another

Act Five

Scene **1**

A street in Mantua
Enter ROMEO

ROMEO   If I may trust the flattering truth of sleep,
          My dreams presage some joyful news at hand.
          My bosom's lord sits lightly in his throne;
          And all this day an unaccustomed spirit
          Lifts me above the ground with cheerful thoughts.   5
          I dreamt my lady came and found me dead –
          Strange dream that gives a dead man leave to think –
          And breathed such life with kisses in my lips,
          That I revived, and was an emperor.
          Ah me, how sweet is love itself possessed,   10
          When but love's shadows are so rich in joy.

          Enter BALTHASAR *his man, booted*

          News from Verona. How now Balthasar,
          Dost thou not bring me letters from the Friar?
          How doth my lady? Is my father well?
          How doth my Juliet? That I ask again,   15
          For nothing can be ill if she be well.

BALTHASAR Then she is well and nothing can be ill.
          Her body sleeps in Capel's monument,
          And her immortal part with angels lives.
          I saw her laid low in her kindred's vault,   20
          And presently took post to tell it you.
          O pardon me for bringing these ill news,
          Since you did leave it for my office sir.

ROMEO   Is it even so? Then I defy you, stars.
          Thou knowest my lodging, get me ink and paper,   25
          And hire post-horses; I will hence tonight.

After telling Romeo that there is no message from Friar Lawrence, Balthasar leaves. Romeo speaks alone. He has decided to kill himself. He knows an apothecary (a chemist) who is very poor and can therefore be persuaded to sell him some poison, although this is illegal.

28	**import** foretell
35	**Let's see for means** Now, how can I do it?
37	**apothecary** a chemist, a person who prepared medicines and other drugs
39	**weeds** clothes
	overwhelming brows overhanging eyebrows
40	**Culling of simples** collecting medicinal herbs
	meagre thin
42	**needy** it was the shop of a poor man
45	**account** collection
46	**earthen** earthenware, terracotta
	bladders containers for liquids
47	**packthread** thread
	cakes of roses rose petals compressed into cakes for use as perfume
49	**penury** poverty
51	**present death** summary execution – if you were caught selling it you were immediately put to death
52	**caitiff** miserable
53	**forerun** come before

BALTHASAR	I do beseech you sir, have patience. Your looks are pale and wild, and do import Some misadventure.
ROMEO	Tush, thou art deceived. Leave me, and do the thing I bid thee do. 30 Hast thou no letters to me from the friar?
BALTHASAR	No my good lord.
ROMEO	No matter. Get thee gone, And hire those horses; I'll be with thee straight.

[*Exit* BALTHASAR

Well, Juliet, I will lie with thee tonight.
Let's see for means. O mischief thou art swift   35
To enter in the thought of desperate men.
I do remember an apothecary –
And hereabouts 'a dwells – which late I noted,
In tattered weeds, with overwhelming brows
Culling of simples; meagre were his looks,   40
Sharp misery had worn him to the bones;
And in his needy shop a tortoise hung,
An alligator stuffed, and other skins
Of ill-shaped fishes, and about his shelves
A beggarly account of empty boxes,   45
Green earthen pots, bladders, and musty seeds,
Remnants of packthread, and old cakes of roses,
Were thinly scattered, to make up a show.
Noting this penury, to myself I said,
'An if a man did need a poison now,   50
Whose sale is present death in Mantua,
Here lives a caitiff wretch would sell it him'.
O this same thought did but forerun my need,
And this same needy man must sell it me.
As I remember, this should be the house.   55
Being holy day, the beggar's shop is shut.
What ho, apothecary!

Enter APOTHECARY

He finds the apothecary and persuades him to sell the poison. The apothecary tells him that the poison he has sold him is strong enough to kill twenty men. Romeo accepts the poison and goes.

59   **ducat** a gold coin: Romeo is offering him a lot of money.

60   **dram** literally 4.5 ml, but just a small dose

        soon-speeding gear rapidly acting substance

63   **trunk** body

63–5   **that ... womb** so that all the breath comes out of my body as violently as the discharge of a gun

65   **womb** interior

67   **utters** sells

68–9   **Art thou ... die?** Can you be so poor and wretched but still afraid of death?

70   **starveth in thy eyes** show in your starving face

73–4   **The world ... it** there are no laws in the world that will make you a rich man, so break the law and become rich that way

75   **My poverty ... consents** I accept because I am so poor, not because I want to

79   **dispatch you straight** kill you immediately

80–2   **gold ... sell** Romeo says that gold poisons men's minds and does far more damage than the poisons that the apothecary is forbidden to sell.

84   **in flesh** in a healthy condition

85   **cordial** medicine or other drink taken to make a person better

APOTHECARY	Who calls so loud?
ROMEO	Come hither man. I see that thou art poor.
	Hold, there is forty ducats, lct me have
	A dram of poison, such soon-speeding gear 60
	As will disperse itself through all the veins,
	That the life-weary taker may fall dead,
	And that the trunk may be discharged of breath,
	As violently as hasty powder fired
	Doth hurry from the fatal cannon's womb. 65
APOTHECARY	Such mortal drugs I have, but Mantua's law
	Is death to any he that utters them.
ROMEO	Art thou so bare and full of wretchedness,
	And fearest to die? Famine is in thy cheeks,
	Need and oppression starveth in thy eyes, 70
	Contempt and beggary hangs upon thy back.
	The world is not thy friend, nor the world's law,
	The world affords no law to make thee rich;
	Then be not poor, but break it, and take this.
APOTHECARY	My poverty, but not my will consents. 75
ROMEO	I pay thy poverty and not thy will.
APOTHECARY	Put this in any liquid thing you will
	And drink it off, and if you had the strength
	Of twenty men, it would dispatch you straight.
ROMEO	There is thy gold, worse poison to men's souls, 80
	Doing more murder in this loathsome world,
	Than these poor compounds that thou mayst not sell.
	I sell thee poison, thou hast sold me none.
	Farewell, buy food, and get thyself in flesh.
	Come cordial, and not poison, go with me 85
	To Juliet's grave, for there must I use thee.

[Exeunt

In Verona Friar Lawrence is visited by Friar John from Mantua. John tells him that there has been an outbreak of plague in Mantua and so he has been unable to deliver Friar Lawrence's letter to Romeo. Lawrence prepares to go to the Capulets' tomb immediately to rescue Juliet.

4	**if ... writ**	if he's written his thoughts down
5–8	**Going ... finding him**	I went to look for a friar of our order to accompany me; I found him visiting the sick here in this city
5	**bare-foot**	May mean literally without shoes but it was also a term for a friar wearing sandals rather than shoes.
8	**the searchers**	officials whose task was to examine dead bodies and decide on the cause of death
9–10	**Suspecting ... reign**	these men thought we were in a house where we might have been infected by the plague
11	**would ... forth**	would not allow us to continue our journey
12	**stayed**	delayed
13	**bare**	carried
15	**Nor get**	neither could I get
18	**nice**	trivial
	full of charge	of vital importance
19	**dear import**	considerable concern
21	**crow**	crowbar
23	**monument**	Juliet's tomb
25	**beshrew me much**	blame me a lot
26	**Hath ... accidents**	has not been told of all these events

Scene ❷

Friar Lawrence's cell
Enter FRIAR JOHN

F. JOHN   Holy Franciscan friar, brother, ho!

Enter FRIAR LAWRENCE

F. LAWRENCE   This same should be the voice of Friar John.
Welcome from Mantua. What says Romeo?
Or if his mind be writ, give me his letter.

F. JOHN   Going to find a bare-foot brother out,   5
One of our order, to associate me,
Here in this city visiting the sick,
And finding him, the searchers of the town,
Suspecting that we both were in a house
Where the infectious pestilence did reign,   10
Sealed up the doors, and would not let us forth,
So that my speed to Mantua there was stayed.

F. LAWRENCE   Who bare my letter then to Romeo?

F. JOHN   I could not send it, here it is again –
Nor get a messenger to bring it thee,   15
So fearful were they of infection.

F. LAWRENCE   Unhappy fortune! By my brotherhood,
The letter was not nice, but full of charge
Of dear import; and the neglecting it
May do much danger. Friar John, go hence,   20
Get me an iron crow and bring it straight
Unto my cell.

F. JOHN   Brother I'll go and bring it thee.

[Exit

F. LAWRENCE   Now must I to the monument alone;
Within this three hours will fair Juliet wake.
She will beshrew me much that Romeo   25
Hath had no notice of these accidents.

29   **corse** corpse

Paris arrives at Juliet's tomb accompanied by his Page. Sending the Page to keep watch he lays flowers on the grave and speaks of his grief at Juliet's death. The Page warns him that someone is coming and he hides.

1   **aloof** some distance away

2   **I would ... seen** I don't want anyone to see me

3   **all along** flat on the ground

5–7   **So shall ... hear it** The ground has been so disturbed by digging graves that it will be easy to hear the vibration of people's footsteps

12   **Sweet flower** He is speaking to Juliet.

14   **sweet water** perfumed water

15   **distilled** forced out

16   **obsequies** memorial ceremony

20   **cross** interrupt

       rite ceremony

21   **Muffle ... awhile** He asks the night to hide him for a while.

But I will write again to Mantua,
And keep her at my cell till Romeo come –
Poor living corse closed in a dead man's tomb.

[*Exit*

Scene ❸

A churchyard, outside the tomb of the Capulets
Enter PARIS *and his* PAGE *with flowers and sweet*
water

PARIS	Give me thy torch boy. Hence, and stand aloof.
	Yet put it out, for I would not be seen.
	Under yond yew trees lay thee all along,
	Holding thy ear close to the hollow ground;
	So shall no foot upon the churchyard tread, 5
	Being loose, unfirm, with digging up of graves,
	But thou shalt hear it; whistle then to me,
	As signal that thou hearest something approach.
	Give me those flowers. Do as I bid thee, go.
PAGE	I am almost afraid to stand alone 10
	Here in the churchyard, yet I will adventure.

[PARIS *strews the tomb with flowers*

PARIS	Sweet flower, with flowers thy bridal bed I strew.
	O woe, thy canopy is dust and stones,
	Which with sweet water nightly I will dew,
	Or wanting that, with tears distilled by moans. 15
	The obsequies that I for thee will keep,
	Nightly shall be to strew thy grave and weep.

[PAGE *whistles*

The boy gives warning something doth approach.
What cursed foot wanders this way tonight,
To cross my obsequies and true love's rite?   20
What, with a torch? Muffle me night a while.

[*Retires*

It is Romeo with his servant Balthasar. Romeo takes the tools Balthasar is carrying and, after giving him a letter for his father, tells him to go. Balthasar says he will, but only goes just out of sight because he is worried about what Romeo will do. Romeo starts to open Juliet's tomb, but Paris comes out of his hiding-place and tries to stop him.

22	**mattock** pickaxe
	wrenching iron crowbar
25	**charge** order, command
26	**aloof** some distance away
27	**in my course** in what I am doing
30–1	**But ... precious ring** Romeo gives this as his excuse for wanting to open Juliet's tomb.
32	**In dear employment** for a purpose that is very important to me
33	**jealous** suspicious
38	**inexorable** relentless
39	**empty** hungry
43	**For ... same** In spite of what he says
44	**his intents I doubt** I am worried about what he is planning to do
45	**maw** stomach
46	**Gorged ... earth** Romeo imagines the tomb as a monster that has devoured the most precious mouthful in the world.
48	**I'll cram ... food** He is going to kill himself and provide more 'food' for the grave.

Enter ROMEO *and* BALTHASAR *with a torch, a*
mattock, and a crow of iron

ROMEO   Give me that mattock and the wrenching-iron.
Hold, take this letter. Early in the morning
See thou deliver it to my lord and father.
Give me the light. Upon thy life I charge thee,   25
Whate'er thou hearest or seest, stand all aloof,
And do not interrupt me in my course.
Why I descend into this bed of death,
Is partly to behold my lady's face;
But chiefly to take thence from her dead finger   30
A precious ring, a ring that I must use
In dear employment. Therefore hence, be gone.
But if thou, jealous, dost return to pry
In what I farther shall intend to do,
By heaven I will tear thee joint by joint,   35
And strew this hungry churchyard with thy limbs.
The time and my intents are savage-wild,
More fierce and more inexorable far
Than empty tigers, or the roaring sea.

BALTHASAR   I will be gone sir, and not trouble you.   40

ROMEO   So shalt thou show me friendship. Take thou that.
Live and be prosperous, and farewell good fellow.

BALTHASAR   [*Aside*] For all this same, I'll hide me hereabout.
His looks I fear, and his intents I doubt.

                            [*Retires*

ROMEO   Thou detestable maw, thou womb of death,   45
Gorged with the dearest morsel of the earth,
Thus I enforce thy rotten jaws to open,

                        [*Opens the tomb*

And in despite I'll cram thee with more food.

PARIS   This is that banished haughty Montague,
That murdered my love's cousin, with which
        grief   50
It is supposed the fair creature died,

Romeo tells him that he is desperate and that Paris should not tempt his anger, but Paris persists. They fight and Paris is killed. It is only then that Romeo realises who he has killed and why he was there. He proceeds to open the tomb and, as Paris had requested before he died, places the body of Paris beside Juliet.

54	**unhallowed toil** unholy work
56	**apprehend** arrest
65	**armed against myself** He only has a weapon because he is going to kill himself.
68	**conjuration** appeal
69	**felon** criminal
74	**peruse** look at
76	**betossed** disturbed
77	**Did ... rode** was not paying attention during the journey here
82	**One ... book** He sees Paris as someone like himself, destined to be unfortunate.

	And here is come to do some villainous shame	
	To the dead bodies. I will apprehend him.	
	Stop thy unhallowed toil, vile Montague.	
	Can vengeance be pursued further than death?	55
	Condemned villain, I do apprehend thee.	
	Obey and go with me, for thou must die.	
ROMEO	I must indeed, and therefore came I hither.	
	Good gentle youth, tempt not a desperate man;	
	Fly hence and leave me; think upon these	
	gone;	60
	Let them affright thee. I beseech thee youth,	
	Put not another sin upon my head,	
	By urging me to fury. O be gone.	
	By heaven, I love thee better than myself,	
	For I come hither armed against myself.	65
	Stay not, be gone, live, and hereafter say,	
	A madman's mercy bid thee run away.	
PARIS	I do defy thy conjuration,	
	And apprehend thee for a felon here.	
ROMEO	Wilt thou provoke me? Then have at thee boy.	70

[*They fight*

PAGE	O Lord, they fight! I will go call the watch.	[*Exit*
PARIS	O I am slain. If thou be merciful,	
	Open the tomb, lay me with Juliet.	
ROMEO	In faith I will. Let me peruse this face.	
	Mercutio's kinsman, noble County Paris!	75
	What said my man, when my betossed soul	
	Did not attend him as we rode? I think	
	He told me Paris should have married Juliet.	
	Said he not so? Or did I dream it so?	
	Or am I mad, hearing him talk of Juliet,	80
	To think it was so? O give me thy hand,	
	One writ with me in sour misfortune's book.	
	I'll bury thee in a triumphant grave.	
	A grave? O no, a lantern, slaughtered youth;	
	For here lies Juliet, and her beauty makes	85

Romeo is struck by Juliet's beauty. Swearing that he will stay with her forever, he swallows the poison and dies.

87   **by ... interred** Literally, buried by a dead man. Romeo is going to kill himself and sees himself as already dead.

90   **lightning** lightening – becoming brighter, more cheerful

94   **ensign** flag carried in battle: Romeo is talking about the battle between life and death for possession of Juliet's body.

100   **sunder** cut

103   **unsubstantial ... amorous** bodiless death is in love (with Juliet)

104   **abhorred** that we shrink from in horror

105   **paramour** lover

111   **shake ... stars** shake off the burden imposed by fate

114–15 seal ... death make an eternal bargain with death that wants to take possession of our lives and seal with a kiss

116–18 Come bitter ... bark Romeo compares his willpower to the pilot and his body to the boat which is being steered onto the rocks of death.

This vault a feasting presence full of light.
Death, lie thou there, by a dead man interred.

[*Lays* PARIS *in the monument*

How oft when men are at the point of death
Have they been merry, which their keepers call
A lightning before death. O how may I   90
Call this a lightning? O my love, my wife!
Death that hath sucked the honey of thy breath
Hath had no power yet upon thy beauty.
Thou art not conquered; beauty's ensign yet
Is crimson in thy lips and in thy cheeks,   95
And death's pale flag is not advanced there.
Tybalt, liest thou there in thy bloody sheet?
O what more favour can I do to thee,
Than with that hand that cut thy youth in twain
To sunder his that was thine enemy?   100
Forgive me cousin. Ah dear Juliet,
Why art thou yet so fair? Shall I believe
That unsubstantial death is amorous,
And that the lean abhorred monster keeps
Thee here in dark to be his paramour?   105
For fear of that, I still will stay with thee,
And never from this palace of dim night
Depart again. Here, here will I remain
With worms that are thy chamber-maids. O here
Will I set up my everlasting rest;   110
And shake the yoke of inauspicious stars
From this world-wearied flesh. Eyes look your last.
Arms, take your last embrace. And lips, O you
The doors of breath, seal with a righteous kiss
A dateless bargain to engrossing death.   115
[*Takes out the poison*] Come bitter conduct, come
    unsavoury guide.
Thou desperate pilot, now at once run on
The dashing rocks thy sea-sick weary bark.
Here's to my love! [*drinks*] O true apothecary!
Thy drugs are quick. Thus with a kiss I die.   120

Nearby, Friar Lawrence, hurrying towards the tomb, meets Balthasar, who tells him that Romeo is already there. The Friar finds the bodies of Romeo and Paris.

121	**be my speed** help me to hurry
124	**Bliss** Blessings
125	**yond** that one over there
125–6	**that vainly ... skulls** that pointlessly lights up worms and skulls
126	**As I discern** As far as I can see
134	**his intents** what he was planning to do
136	**some ... thing** some evil harmful thing
141	**sepulchre** burial place
142	**masterless** They have been thrown down and so have no 'masters'.
	gory bloody
145	**steeped** soaked
145–6	**Ah ... chance** What unnatural moment led to this sorrowful event

Enter FRIAR LAWRENCE, *with lantern, crow and spade*

F. LAWRENCE	Saint Francis be my speed. How oft tonight Have my old feet stumbled at graves. Who's there?
BALTHASAR	Here's one, a friend, and one that knows you well.
F. LAWRENCE	Bliss be upon you. Tell me, good my friend. What torch is yond, that vainly lends his light 125 To grubs and eyeless skulls? As I discern, It burneth in the Capels' monument.
BALTHASAR	It doth so holy sir, and there's my master, One that you love.
F. LAWRENCE	Who is it?
BALTHASAR	Romeo.
F. LAWRENCE	How long hath he been there?
BALTHASAR	Full half an hour. 130
F. LAWRENCE	Go with me to the vault.
BALTHASAR	I dare not sir. My master knows not but I am gone hence; And fearfully did menace me with death, If I did stay to look on his intents.
F. LAWRENCE	Stay then, I'll go alone. Fear comes upon me. 135 O much I fear some ill unthrifty thing.
BALTHASAR	As I did sleep under this yew tree here, I dreamt my master and another fought, And that my master slew him.
F. LAWRENCE	Romeo!

       [*Stoops and looks on the blood and weapons*

       Alack, alack, what blood is this which stains 140
       The stony entrance of this sepulchre?
       What mean these masterless and gory swords
       To lie discoloured by this place of peace?

              [*Enters the monument*

       Romeo! O pale! Who else! What, Paris too?
       And steeped in blood? Ah what an unkind hour 145
       Is guilty of this lamentable chance!

At this moment Juliet begins to wake up. Friar Lawrence tells her what has happened and tries to hurry her away because he has heard a noise but Juliet refuses to leave. Afraid of what may happen, he goes. Juliet sees that Romeo has poisoned himself. Hearing people coming she takes Romeo's dagger and kills herself. Led by Paris's Page, the Watchmen discover the bodies of Romeo, Juliet and Paris.

148   **comfortable** comforting, reassuring

152   **contagion** poisonous influences

155   **in thy bosom** As he died, Romeo must have fallen across Juliet's sleeping body.

157   **sisterhood ... nuns** a nunnery

162   **hath ... end** has killed him

163   **churl** ill-mannered person (but Juliet is saying it affectionately)

165   **Haply** perhaps

166   **restorative** She kisses him (which in fairy tales would restore him to life).

172   **attach** arrest

The lady stirs. [JULIET *rises*

JULIET   O comfortable Friar, where is my lord?
I do remember well where I should be,
And there I am. Where is my Romeo?   150

[*Noise within*

F. LAWRENCE   I hear some noise. Lady, come from that nest
Of death, contagion, and unnatural sleep,
A greater power than we can contradict
Hath thwarted our intents. Come, come away.
Thy husband in thy bosom there lies dead;   155
And Paris too. Come I'll dispose of thee
Among a sisterhood of holy nuns.
Stay not to question, for the watch is coming.
Come, go good Juliet, I dare no longer stay.

[*Exit* FRIAR LAWRENCE

JULIET   Go get thee hence, for I will not away.   160
What's here? A cup closed in my true love's hand?
Poison I see hath been his timeless end.
O churl, drunk all, and left no friendly drop
To help me after? I will kiss thy lips;
Haply some poison yet doth hang on them,   165
To make me die with a restorative.
Thy lips are warm.

1ST WATCH   [*Within*]   Lead, boy. Which way?

JULIET   Yea, noise? Then I'll be brief. O happy dagger!

[*Draws* ROMEO's *dagger*

This is thy sheath; there rest, and let me die.

[*She stabs herself*

Enter WATCH, *with the* PAGE *of* PARIS

PAGE   This is the place; there where the torch doth
burn.   170

1ST WATCH   The ground is bloody, search about the churchyard.
Go some of you, whoe'er you find attach.

[*Exeunt some of the* WATCH

Pitiful sight! Here lies the County slain,

Another Watchman has arrested Friar Lawrence and brings him back to the tomb. They are followed by the Prince and the Capulets, who express their horror at the sight before them.

178–80 We see ... descry a **play on words** (see Glossary p. 291): 'Ground' means 1) the place where the bodies are 2) the reason why they are there.

    descry make out

184   **mattock** pickaxe

187   **misadventure** unfortunate event

And Juliet bleeding, warm, and newly dead,
Who here hath lain this two days buried.   175
Go tell the Prince, run to the Capulets,
Raise up the Montagues, some others search.

[Exeunt others of the WATCH

We see the ground whereon these woes do lie,
But the true ground of all these piteous woes
We cannot without circumstance descry.   180

Enter some of the WATCH *with* BALTHASAR

2ND WATCH   Here's Romeo's man, we found him in the
             churchyard.

1ST WATCH   Hold him in safety, till the Prince come hither.

Enter FRIAR LAWRENCE *with another* WATCHMAN

3RD WATCH   Here is a friar that trembles, sighs, and weeps.
             We took this mattock and this spade from him,
             As he was coming from this churchyard's side.   185

1ST WATCH   A great suspicion. Stay the friar too.

Enter the PRINCE *and Attendants*

PRINCE   What misadventure is so early up,
             That calls our person from our morning rest?

Enter CAPULET *and* LADY CAPULET

CAPULET   What should it be that is so shrieked abroad?

L. CAPULET   The people in the street cry 'Romeo';   190
             Some 'Juliet', and some 'Paris', and all run
             With open outcry toward our monument.

PRINCE   What fear is this which startles in your ears?

1ST WATCH   Sovereign, here lies the County Paris slain,
             And Romeo dead, and Juliet, dead before,   195
             Warm and new killed.

PRINCE   Search, seek, and know how this foul murder
             comes.

Montague arrives on the scene, explains that his wife has died and expresses his grief at his son's death. At the Prince's command, Friar Lawrence begins to explain the sequence of events that has led to the tragedy.

198   **man** servant

202–4   **lo his ... bosom** The scabbard Romeo wore is empty and the dagger has wrongly been 'sheathed' in Juliet's body.

205–6   **this sight ... sepulchre** seeing these dead bodies is like a church bell calling me to my own funeral

208   **down** dead

209   **my liege** my lord

213   **untaught** Romeo has not learned his manners and has pushed in front of his father to die before him.

215   **Seal ... outrage** Calm these violent expressions of grief: the Prince's words can also express the outrage felt at the violent opening of the tomb.

217   **And know ... descent** and determine their source, their origin, how they came to be

218   **be ... woes** lead the investigation into this grief

219   **even to death** even to the death penalty if need be

220   **let ... patience** allow patience to be the master of this misfortune

222   **the greatest** the one under most suspicion

224   **make** witness

225   **impeach and purge** accuse and excuse

226   **Myself ... excused** my guilt and my innocence

228–9   **my ... tedious tale** the time I have left to me is shorter than a painful story

1ST WATCH	Here is a friar, and slaughtered Romeo's man,
	With instruments upon them, fit to open
	These dead men's tombs. 200
CAPULET	O heavens! O wife, look how our daughter bleeds.
	This dagger has mista'en, for lo his house
	Is empty on the back of Montague,
	And is mis-sheathed in my daughter's bosom.
L. CAPULET	O me, this sight of death is as a bell, 205
	That warns my old age to a sepulchre.

Enter MONTAGUE

PRINCE	Come Montague, for thou art early up,
	To see thy son and heir more early down.
MONTAGUE	Alas my liege, my wife is dead tonight.
	Grief of my son's exile hath stopped her breath. 210
	What further woe conspires against mine age?
PRINCE	Look and thou shalt see.
MONTAGUE	O thou untaught, what manners is in this,
	To press before thy father to a grave?
PRINCE	Seal up the mouth of outrage for a while, 215
	Till we can clear these ambiguities,
	And know their spring, their head, their true
	descent;
	And then will I be general of your woes,
	And lead you even to death. Meantime forbear,
	And let mischance be slave to patience. 220
	Bring forth the parties of suspicion.
F. LAWRENCE	I am the greatest, able to do least,
	Yet most suspected, as the time and place
	Doth make against me, of this direful murder.
	And here I stand both to impeach and purge 225
	Myself condemned, and myself excused.
PRINCE	Then say at once what thou dost know in this.
F. LAWRENCE	I will be brief, for my short date of breath
	Is not so long as is a tedious tale.
	Romeo, there dead, was husband to that Juliet; 230

Friar Lawrence explains the sequence of events that has led to the tragedy.

232 **stolen marriage-day** 'Stolen' because they took it secretly, although it was not allowed.

233 **untimely** mistimed

235 **For whom ... Juliet** Juliet was languishing in grief for Romeo, not for Tybalt.

236–8 **You, to remove ... Paris** You, in order, as you thought, to take away this attack of grief, had her engaged to Count Paris and intended to marry her forcibly to him

239 **bid ... mean** begged me to think of some way

242 **so ... art** my studies having taught me this

244–5 **it wrought ... death** it made her look exactly as though she was dead

246 **That he ... night** that he should come here as indeed he did on this fatal night

248 **Being the time** since this was the time

250 **stayed** held back

253 **her kindred's vault** the family's burial chamber (This would contain individual graves of family members.)

254 **closely** secretly

256 **ere** before

257 **untimely** before their time

258 **true** faithful, loyal

259 **entreated ... forth** begged her to come away

260 **work of heaven** what heaven had decreed

263 **did ... herself** killed herself

264–5 **to the ... privy** the Nurse knows about the marriage

265 **aught** anything

266–8 **Miscarried ... law** Friar Lawrence says that if he is at fault he is willing to die, as the law demands.

And she, there dead, that Romeo's faithful wife.
I married them, and their stolen marriage-day
Was Tybalt's dooms-day, whose untimely death
Banished the new-made bridegroom from this city;
For whom, and not for Tybalt, Juliet pined.   235
You, to remove that siege of grief from her,
Betrothed, and would have married her perforce,
To County Paris. Then comes she to me,
And, with wild looks, bid me devise some mean
To rid her from this second marriage,   240
Or in my cell there would she kill herself.
Then gave I her, so tutored by my art,
A sleeping potion, which so took effect
As I intended, for it wrought on her
The form of death. Meantime I writ to Romeo,   245
That he should hither come as this dire night,
To help to take her from her borrowed grave,
Being the time the potion's force should cease.
But he which bore my letter, Friar John,
Was stayed by accident, and yesternight   250
Returned my letter back. Then all alone
At the prefixed hour of her waking,
Came I to take her from her kindred's vault,
Meaning to keep her closely at my cell,
Till I conveniently could send to Romeo.   255
But when I came, some minute ere the time
Of her awakening, here untimely lay
The noble Paris and true Romeo dead.
She wakes, and I entreated her come forth,
And bear this work of heaven with patience.   260
But then a noise did scare me from the tomb,
And she, too desperate, would not go with me,
But, as it seems, did violence on herself.
All this I know, and to the marriage
Her Nurse is privy; and if aught in this   265
Miscarried by my fault, let my old life

Further details are supplied by Balthasar, who gives the Prince Romeo's letter, and by Paris's Page. The Prince reads the letter which confirms the Friar's story. Capulet and Montague realise that it is their feud which has led to the tragedy and they agree to abandon all hostility. They will raise statues of Romeo and Juliet as a memorial to their children and to show that the two families are now at peace.

269	**We still … man** We have always recognised you to be a holy man
272	**in post** in haste
275	**going in** as he went in
278	**raised the Watch** alerted the watchman
279	**what … master** what was your master doing
280	**strew** scatter on
281	**aloof** apart
282	**comes … light** someone comes with a lantern
283	**drew on him** drew his sword to threaten him
286	**tidings** news
288	**pothecary** apothecary
	therewithal with it
291	**scourge** punishment
	laid upon caused by
293	**winking at** turning a blind eye to
294	**a brace of kinsmen** Paris and Mercutio were both relatives of the Prince.
296	**jointure** marriage settlement, money and goods given by the groom's family to the bride at the time of the wedding
299	**whiles** as long as
300	**There … set** no statue shall ever be as highly valued

	Be sacrificed some hour before his time, Unto the rigour of severest law.	
PRINCE	We still have known thee for a holy man. Where's Romeo's man? What can he say to this?	270
BALTHASAR	I brought my master news of Juliet's death, And then in post he came from Mantua To this same place, to this same monument. This letter he early bid me give his father, And threatened me with death, going in the vault, If I departed not, and left him there.	275
PRINCE	Give me the letter, I will look on it. Where is the County's page, that raised the Watch? Sirrah, what made your master in this place?	
PAGE	He came with flowers to strew his lady's grave, And bid me stand aloof, and so I did. Anon comes one with light to ope the tomb, And by and by my master drew on him, And then I ran away to call the Watch.	280
PRINCE	This letter doth make good the Friar's words, Their course of love, the tidings of her death. And here he writes that he did buy a poison Of a poor pothecary, and therewithal Came to this vault to die and lie with Juliet. Where be these enemies? Capulet, Montague, See what a scourge is laid upon your hate, That heaven finds means to kill your joys with love. And I for winking at your discords too Have lost a brace of kinsmen; all are punished.	285 290
CAPULET	O brother Montague, give me thy hand. This is my daughter's jointure, for no more Can I demand.	295
MONTAGUE	But I can give thee more. For I will raise her statue in pure gold, That whiles Verona by that name is known, There shall no figure at such rate be set	300

304   **glooming** dark

Act 5 scenes 1 to 3

Cutting the text

Romeo and Juliet is quite long, and for modern audiences, the second half of the play can seem to drag. Many directors cut the text in order to speed up the action. Imagine that you are working on a really short version of the play. The first 20 lines of Act 5 scene 1 could be cut to just six:

ROMEO   My dreams presage some joyful news at hand.
          Ah me, how sweet is love itself possessed,
          When but love's shadows are so rich in joy.

          Enter BALTHASAR

          How now Balthasar, how doth my lady?

BALTHASAR Her body sleeps in Capels' monument,
          And her immortal part with angels lives.

Work on your own

1   Work on the rest of the scene and cut it in a similar way.

	As that of true and faithful Juliet.
CAPULET	As rich shall Romeo by his lady lie,
	Poor sacrifices of our enmity.
PRINCE	A glooming peace this morning with it brings;
	The sun for sorrow will not show his head. 305
	Go hence to have more talk of these sad things;
	Some shall be pardoned, and some punished.
	For never was a story of more woe
	Than this of Juliet and her Romeo.

[*Exeunt*

ACTIVITIES

Work with a partner

2 Compare your two versions. Agree on a shared version.

Work in a group of four

3 Now look at scenes 2 and 3. Imagine that you are preparing a film of the play and that you have been told to cut these two scenes down to no more than 150 lines. Decide how you will cut the text, and think about how you will use film to tell the story. You could:

   a use visuals to tell part of the story

   b cut whole characters or sections of action.

   You need to think about:

   c What are the essential dramatic elements of the scene?

   d Which lines will have the biggest impact on the audience?

4 Prepare a presentation for the rest of the class.

   a Read the cut version of the script.

   b Have one member of the group explaining the film effects you have worked out.

Death imagery

Romeo's language in Act 5 scene 3 is full of startling imagery of death.

Line 28: 'this bed of death'
Line 36: 'this hungry churchyard'
Line 45: Juliet's tomb is 'thou detestable maw' (*stomach*)
Line 45: Juliet's tomb is 'thou womb of death'

Here is the start of a mind map to explore one of these images:

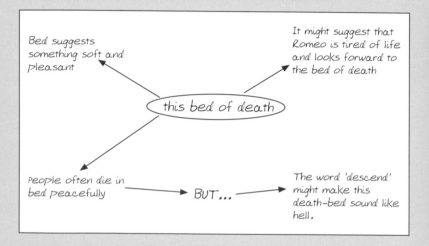

Work in a group of four

1 Use large sheets of paper to build up mind maps exploring two of the other death images listed above.

2 Find at least two more death images used by Romeo later in the scene. Use mind maps to explore the possible effects of those images.

3 Discuss an answer to this question:
   What does Romeo's use of language in this scene suggest about his attitudes and feelings towards death?

4 Prepare to present your answer to the rest of the class.

Plot summary quiz

The 12 short quotations below sum up the story of Act 5.

1 Work out the correct order for them.

2 Work out who said each of them.

A

Thus with a kiss I die.

B

Well, Juliet, I will lie with thee tonight.

C

This is that banished haughty Montague, That murdered my love's cousin...

D

Sweet flower, with flowers thy bridal bed I strew.

E

O comfortable friar, where is my lord?

F

I sell thee poison, thou hast sold me none.

G

Wilt thou provoke me? Then have at thee boy.

H

Ah dear Juliet, Why art thou yet so fair?

I

Some shall be pardoned and some punished.

J

I saw her laid low in her kindred's vault...

K

I dreamt my lady came and found me dead...

L

O churl, drunk all, and left no friendly drop To help me after?

Act 1

The latest street fighting between the Capulets and Montagues ends when the Prince of Verona arrives and threatens to execute anyone who continues fighting. To help Romeo get over being rejected by the girl he loves, his friends persuade him to join them in gate-crashing the Capulets' party. Juliet's cousin, Tybalt, recognises Romeo at the party and wants him thrown out because he is a Montague. Lord Capulet humiliates Tybalt by ordering him to leave Romeo alone. Juliet's parents want her to marry Count Paris, but when Romeo and Juliet meet at the party they fall in love. To their horror, they discover they are from opposing families.

Act 2

After the party, Romeo gives his friends the slip and enters the Capulets' garden where he sees Juliet on her balcony. He surprises her, they express their love for each other and decide to marry in secret the next day. Friar Lawrence agrees to marry Romeo and Juliet in the hope that this will unite their families. Romeo sends Juliet the wedding details via her Nurse (who has looked after her since birth). Juliet slips out of her house, joins Romeo and they are married.

Act 3

When Romeo refuses to fight Tybalt in the street, Tybalt fights and kills Mercutio. This provokes Romeo into killing Tybalt. The Prince exiles Romeo as punishment. Distraught, Romeo seeks the advice of Friar Lawrence, who tells him to hide in Mantua. Juliet is horrified when she hears Romeo has killed her cousin, but soon takes her husband's side. She sends the Nurse to bring Romeo to her. Romeo and Juliet secretly spend the night together. In the morning Juliet's parents shock and anger Juliet with the news that she must marry Paris later that week. The Nurse advises Juliet to marry Paris.

Act 4

Friar Lawrence gives Juliet a potion that will make her seem dead. He tells her he will send for Romeo to rescue her secretly from her tomb. Juliet goes home and tells her parents she will obey them and marry Paris. However, she drinks the potion and on her wedding morning Juliet's parents find that she is 'dead'. They are grief-stricken. Friar Lawrence advises them to bury her immediately.

Act 5

Romeo hears that Juliet is dead. Friar Lawrence's message of explanation doesn't get through to Romeo. Romeo buys poison to kill himself. He rushes to Juliet's tomb, where he meets and kills Paris. Inside the tomb he poisons himself next to Juliet, who then wakes up, finds Romeo's body and stabs herself to death. The Prince hears what has happened and promises to pardon some and punish others.

Act/ Scene	Action	Theme/Summary
Prologue	Introduction to the tragedy.	Fate, feuds, love and death.
1.1	Montagues and Capulets fight. Romeo is love-sick.	Painful love. Love and hate.
1.2	Romeo reluctantly agrees to go to the Capulet party.	Romeo's love for Rosaline.
1.3	Her mother urges Juliet to marry Count Paris.	Love, marriage and sex.
1.4	Mercutio urges Romeo not to give in to the misery of love.	The effects of love.
1.5	Romeo and Juliet fall in love.	Love at first sight.
2.1	Romeo escapes his friends.	Mercutio's crude talk.
2.2	The balcony scene.	Romantic love.
2.3	A marriage is arranged.	Love and reconciliation.
2.4	Romeo arranges to marry Juliet.	Mercutio's continuing scorn.
2.5	Nurse reports back to Juliet.	Nurse as comic character.
2.6	The secret wedding.	Love with holy blessing.
3.1	Mercutio and Tybalt killed in street fight. Romeo banished.	Violence, manliness, justice.
3.2	Juliet forgives Romeo.	Loyal love.
3.3	Friar Lawrence advises Romeo.	Manliness. The Friar's wisdom.
3.4	Capulet promises Juliet to Paris.	A father's power.
3.5	Romeo and Juliet sleep together. Juliet refuses to marry Paris.	Romantic love. Rebellion against parental authority.
4.1	Friar Lawrence's potion plan.	Friar Lawrence's wisdom.
4.2	Juliet 'gives in' to her parents.	Juliet in control.
4.3	Juliet takes the potion.	Juliet overcomes her fears.
4.4	Preparations for the wedding.	Chaos in Capulet house.
4.5	Juliet found 'dead'.	Parents' grief.
5.1	Romeo hears of Juliet's 'death'.	Romeo decides on suicide.
5.2	Friar Lawrence fails.	Cruel fate.
5.3	Romeo and Juliet kill themselves.	Conflict leads to tragedy.

In this section of the book there are activities and advice to help you explore the play in more detail:

- Character (pages 262–6)
- Drama and performance (pages 268–72)
- Themes and issues (pages 273–81)
- Writing about *Romeo and Juliet* (pages 282–6)
- Writing tasks and questions (pages 286–7)

On pages 288–93 there is a Glossary, which explains some of the technical terms that are used in the book.

Character

Relationships

There are many different relationships in *Romeo and Juliet*. These include:

- father / daughter
- husband / wife
- master / servant
- lovers.

Many relationships are unequal: one side has power over the other. For example, the Prince can punish – and even execute – his subjects.

1 For each of these four types of relationship, write down one example from the play.

2 What other types of relationship can you find in the play?

3 What sort of relationship exists between Friar Lawrence and Romeo?

Character X-ray

To see characters' true thoughts and feelings we need to do a sort of X-ray of their minds.

How to make a character X-ray

Choose one important moment in the play.

1 Around the edge of a large sheet of paper write the names of the characters who are on stage.

2 From each character draw an arrow to the character(s) who they are thinking about.

3 On one side of the arrow write what you think the character's thoughts are; on the other side write their feelings. To do this, think carefully about what you have learned about the characters from:

- what they say and do
- what other characters say about them.

Here is an example from Act 3 scene 1 lines 37–56:

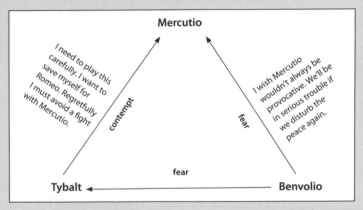

4 Make character X-rays for two other important moments in the play.

Character interpretation

Many different interpretations are brought to bear on a play: first of all the director decides roughly how a character should be 'portrayed'. An actor then works closely with the director to develop that interpretation. Finally, each member of the audience understands the characters in their own way. The Nurse, for example, could be seen as a ridiculous fool or as wise, affectionate and 'put upon' by a rather spoilt and petulant Juliet. Both versions could work.

The best way explore a character is to try them out in different ways. For example, on the following page are alternative performance guidelines for Act 4 scene 1 lines 18–43:

	Version 1	**Version 2**
Juliet	You are 13 years old, but you have a self-confidence that suggests you are much older; you tend to become very emotional very quickly; many of your family think of you as 'hot-headed'; you hate Paris and want him to know it. You are determined not to look Paris in the face.	Paris has been forced on you by your parents. They aren't interested in your happiness – only the money that he will bring with him as a wedding dowry. You want to get rid of him as quickly as possible so that you can ask Friar Lawrence what to do next.
Paris	You are 22 years old. Marriage to Juliet is important because it will ally you to one of the most powerful families around. You have often heard that Juliet is 'difficult', but you believe that firm handling and humouring her will bring her under control. You are determined to smooth talk her whatever she says. You are going to try to kiss her.	You expect Juliet to do as she is told by her parents, so you are rather taken aback when she slaps you down. You are irritated and expect to get your own way: you aren't going to stand for any nonsense. The more she answers back the more annoyed you get: just wait until you are married and then she'll find out who's boss!

Work with a partner

1 Choose a short section of the play. For example, you could try:

   a Act 2 scene 4 lines 144–85

   b Act 3 scene 4.

2 Agree on a few performance guidelines for each character. Perform the section with each of you trying to stick to the performance guidelines for your character.

3 Now agree new performance guidelines and act out the section again. Which guidelines work best? Why? What other guidelines could you have used?

Character development graph

The main characters in *Romeo and Juliet* are changed by their experiences in the course of the play. A character development graph allows you to chart changes in:

- a character
- the relationship between characters
- the way the audience feels about a character.

Here is a simple example: the graph at the top of the next page begins to explore how an audience's feelings towards Lord Capulet might change during the first half of the play.

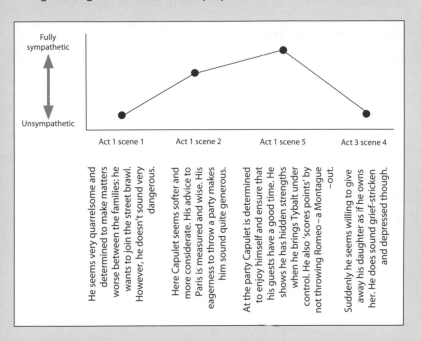

Fully sympathetic

Unsympathetic

Act 1 scene 1 · Act 1 scene 2 · Act 1 scene 5 · Act 3 scene 4

He seems very quarrelsome and determined to make matters worse between the families: he wants to join in the street brawl. However, he doesn't sound very dangerous.

Here Capulet seems softer and more considerate. His advice to Paris is measured and wise. His eagerness to throw a party makes him sound quite generous.

At the party Capulet is determined to enjoy himself and ensure that his guests have a good time. He shows he has hidden strengths when he brings Tybalt under control. He also 'scores points' by not throwing Romeo – a Montague – out.

Suddenly he seems willing to give away his daughter as if he owns her. He does sound grief-stricken and depressed though.

Make character development graphs of your own. Here are some topics worth exploring in detail:

1   The relationship between Romeo and Juliet

2   How sympathetic the audience might find the Nurse.

Important reminder: do not forget that when you do a development graph you are working with your interpretation, and other interpretations are possible. That is why it is better to do this exercise with others who are willing to challenge your interpretations and force you to find evidence to support them.

Close study

We get to know other people by what they say and do, and by how others react to them. The same is true of characters in a play: their words and actions must be carefully studied for clues to what the character is like.

Studying a character

Juliet

1   Make a list of 4–6 character qualities that apply to Juliet.
    For example, you might decide that at different points in the play Juliet is cunning and foolish.

2   Start with the first quality on your list. Search the play for evidence to support this character quality.

3   Make a note of the act, scene, and line numbers for each piece of evidence.

4   Draw a table like the one opposite.

Point	Evidence	Explanation an
Juliet can be cunning and quick-witted	When Juliet talks to her mother about Tybalt's death she deliberately talks at cross-purposes, seeming to condemn Romeo, but in fact meaning that she loves and misses him. (Act 3 scene 5 lines 81–102)	Juliet is in a difficult situation. She doesn't want to lie and agree with her mother. On the other hand, she can't admit to her love for Romeo. So she plays a game with words. For example, she says that 'no man like he [Romeo] doth grieve my heart.' (Act 3 scene 5 line 83) Her mother is bound to interpret this as meaning that Juliet hates Romeo, when in fact her 'grief' is caused by Romeo's absence.

5 Write the character quality in the first column.

6 In the second column write your evidence.

7 In the third column write an explanation of why that evidence supports the point you are making.

8 Now do the same for the other character qualities on your list.

Note: Whenever you can, include a quotation (or the line numbers) as part of your evidence or explanation.

Drama and performance

Thought-tracking

Thought-tracking is a way of exploring characters' thoughts and considering what 'makes them tick'. This is how to do it:

1 Choose a short and important section of the play.

2 Cast the parts, but give each character two actors. One actor should be the 'Character'; the other should play the character's thoughts and feelings (the 'Thought').

3 Each Thought should stand by the shoulder of their Character. The Characters play the scene, but every so often a Thought says 'freeze'.

4 Then the Characters stand still while the Thoughts speak. It is often a good idea to speak the thoughts of the character who has been listening, as well as the one who has been speaking. For example, during Act 3 scene 5 lines 126–204, Lady Capulet is mostly silent, but we know she has strong feelings and opinions. It would be interesting to explore her thoughts during her husband's long speech from line 176 to his exit.

Preparation

If you are a confident group then you could try speaking the thoughts spontaneously (without preparation). However, most people find it useful to prepare by jotting down a few ideas about what a character might be thinking at various points in the scene.

Try out thought-tracking for the following parts of the play:

1 Romeo and Juliet finally part in the balcony scene (Act 2 scene 2 lines 167–85).

2 Capulet promises Juliet to Paris (Act 3 scene 4).

3 Capulet tells Juliet she must marry Paris (Act 3 scene 5 lines 126–76).

Hot-seating

Hot-seating is another way of 'getting inside' a character. It is a good preparation for acting. This is how it works:

1 One member of the class is given a character in a particular scene.

2 The character sits in the 'hot seat' with the class sitting around them in a semi-circle.

3 Class members take it in turns to ask the character in the hot seat questions about how they are feeling, why they said or did certain things, and so on.

4 The pupil in the hot seat has to answer these questions in role and without too much delay. (Their answers can be imaginative but they must make sense in terms of what we know from the play.)

Example: Act 3 scene 1 lines 107–39. Suppose you have been given the role of Romeo. Here are three of the questions you might be asked when you are in the hot seat:

- What did you at first think had happened to Mercutio?
- How did you feel when you realised Mercutio was dead?
- Why didn't you run away as soon as you killed Tybalt?

Tableau

A tableau, or freeze-frame, is like a film with the pause button pressed, so the actors freeze into position at a particular moment. Here's how to do it:

1 One member of your group is the director and helps you all to achieve the agreed expressions and postures.

2 Act out a scene and 'freeze' at different points. Your audience can comment on what each tableau suggests. Photograph the tableau to support further discussion.

3 Prepare freeze-frames for other groups to see and comment on. Their first task is to work out which moment in the play has been frozen.

A tableau can be used in a more abstract way, to express a mood or idea. For example, you might want to express 'love-at-first-sight' in Act 1 scene 5, or 'revenge' in Act 3 scene 1.

Statues and sculptures

At the end of the play Montague promises to have a golden statue of Juliet erected in public. Imagine that other statues are erected at different points in the play – for example, the Prince in Act 1; Tybalt in Act 3; the Nurse at the end of the play.

Work with a partner

1   Work together to sculpt a statue. Choose one character at a particular point in the play (see the previous suggestions).

   a   Decide what feelings and ideas you want this statue to express.

   b   One of you should be the statue.

   c   Together you should decide how the statue should be posed, what expression should be on its face, and so on.

2   Walk round the room looking at other people's statues. Decide who they are statues of, and at what point in the play.

Stepping out of the text

This is another way of exploring characters and 'bringing them to life', this time by wondering what those characters would be like in other situations – even impossible ones.

Some examples of out-of-text situations that you could use:

1   Imagine a school assembly with the Prince as a visiting speaker. What does he say?

2   Imagine that Verona is a sort of reality game-show location. The play's characters are evicted (banished) from the city one by one. Who goes? You decide. Interview each character on their eviction night.

3   What is life like in Verona two years after the end of the play? Work on a scene involving some of the characters.

Remember: Whatever out-of-text activity you use, what the characters say and do must be justified by what we know of them from the play. In other words, they must stay in role.

Decision alley

There is a danger that we simply accept whatever happens in the play as though there were no other possibilities. In fact, playwrights constantly make decisions about what characters will say and do. Decision alley is a method of exploring some of the options that are open to characters (and the playwright) at certain points in the play.

Here is how a decision alley works:

1 One person is cast as the character to be explored.

2 The rest of the class stands in two lines facing each other down the length of the room.

3 Each person in the alley thinks of some brief advice they would like to give the character about what they should do at this point in the play.

4 The character walks slowly down the alley, pausing by each person in the alley.

5 As the character reaches each person, that person speaks their advice. The character listens carefully and thoughtfully.

6 When the person playing the character reaches the end of the alley they should think aloud about the advice they have been given and explain what they have decided to do.

The huge advantage of this technique is that it can involve the whole class and every student can benefit from every other student's thoughts.

'Brave Mercutio is dead'

Decision alley works best for moments in the play when a character is trying to make up their mind.

Try it for Romeo at Act 3 scene 1 line 119 when Romeo realises that Mercutio is dead. How should he react?

Here is the sort of conflicting advice that Romeo might get in the decision alley:

- 'Stay calm. You mustn't let Tybalt provoke you.'
- 'It's unmanly not to take revenge for Mercutio.'

Physical illustration

Sometimes, in film versions of plays, when one character is describing what is happening somewhere else or in the past, we hear their voice over a film of what they are describing. For example, in a film of *Romeo and Juliet* we might hear Friar John's explanation of how he didn't manage to deliver Friar Lawrence's letter while we watch those events happen.

Physical illustration is a version of this.

1 Someone reads a speech from the play.

2 The other members of the group illustrate the speech through actions.

This technique has two main advantages:

- It can keep a long, descriptive speech lively and vivid.
- It helps you to concentrate on the detail of a speech.

'Sailing in this salt flood'

Work in a group of four to six

1 Read again Act 3 scene 5 lines 129–37.

2 In these lines, Capulet describes Juliet as if she were a ship in a storm. Discuss how you might illustrate these metaphors through physical actions.

3 Choose one person in the group to read the lines, while the rest perform your chosen actions.

Follow-up

Another speech you could explore through physical illustration is Act 3 scene 1 lines 155–77, where Benvolio describes the fight that led to Mercutio and Tybalt's deaths.

Themes and issues

Love

We usually think of love as exciting and joyful, but the audience can never fully enjoy the delights of Romeo and Juliet's love because we know from the Prologue that they are 'star-crossed lovers' whose love is 'death-marked'. This connection between love, death and violence is reinforced throughout the play.

Romeo and Juliet's love is too overwhelming, too powerful to be safe, and the way characters refer to love keeps reminding us of this. For example, Romeo calls it 'too rough, | Too rude, too boisterous' (Act 1 scene 4 lines 25–6).

However, 'love' does not just have to mean romantic love. Here are some different sorts of love we come across in the play:

loyalty	family ties	admiration	passion
obsession	close friendships	romance	

Work in a large group

1   Create a tableau for each of the seven types of love listed above. (Tableaux are explained on page 269.) Show some of your tableaux to another group and ask them to work out which type of love each tableau is illustrating.

Work with a partner

2   Find a good example in *Romeo and Juliet* of at least three of the above types of love. Carefully explore these three types of love using a table like the one on the next page.

Type of love	Example	Exploration
Family ties	When Romeo realises that there has been new fighting between the Capulets and Montagues he observes that 'Here's much to do with hate, but more with love.' (Act 1 scene 1 line 174)	Probably Romeo means that the Montagues and Capulets hate each other's families as a way of expressing their love and loyalty to their own family.

Work on your own

3   Look up each of these references to love:

- *Alas that love, so gentle in his view,*
  Should be so tyrannous and rough in proof!
  (Act 1 scene 1 lines 168–9)
- *...o brawling love, o loving hate*
  (Act 1 scene 1 line 175)
- *...we'll draw thee from the mire*
  Of this save-your-reverence love...
  (Act 1 scene 4 lines 41–2)

For each of these three references explain:

a   who said it

b   what type of love it is referring to

c   what it shows about the speaker's attitudes towards love.

The language of love

Work in a small group

4   Shakespeare shows us Romeo and Juliet falling in love at first sight. Their first conversation lasts for only 18 lines and ends with their first kiss. Read these lines again (Act 1 scene 5 lines 92–109). Read the notes on the facing pages, then complete the following tasks:

a Make a list of all the religious words used in these lines.

b What do lines 92–5 tell us about the way in which Romeo thinks of Juliet?

c How does Juliet respond at first (lines 96–9)?

d How does Romeo try to change her mind?

e Why do you think Shakespeare chose to use all these religious images?

f Read lines 92–105 aloud. Notice the rhythm and the rhyming pattern of those 14 lines. (See page 14 for an explanation of a sonnet.) What mood or feeling is created by the way these lines are written?

Fate

The Prologue

Romeo and Juliet is a very romantic play: the central characters fall in passionate love at first sight and are completely devoted to one another. Yet the whole play has an air of doom hanging over it. We are told straight away in the Prologue that the lovers are 'star-crossed' (line 6): in other words, the lovers' stars are in conflict and so their love is inevitably 'death-marked' (line 9).

Work in a group of three
Read the Prologue (page 17) again. Discuss and make notes on the following:

1 List the other words and expressions that tell us that the story of Romeo and Juliet will not end happily.

2 Shakespeare uses a number of words and images to highlight the terrible things that will happen in the play. For example, the conflict between the two families is summed up in line 4: 'Where civil blood makes civil hands unclean'; we get a picture of people with their hands covered with blood. Find two other powerful images and explain why you have chosen them.

3 When we are going to watch a film or play we usually don't want anyone to tell us how it ends. But this is exactly what Shakespeare does here. Why do you think he does this?

Foreshadowing

A tragic fate is gathering around the lovers throughout the play and they are increasingly aware of it: even when they are most in love they fear the worst. This constant signalling of the terrible fate that is waiting for Romeo and Juliet is often called 'foreshadowing': it is like a shadow of the future falling over them as they pursue their love. We see this foreshadowing in Act 1 scene 4 even before the lovers meet: as Romeo prepares to gate-crash the party where he will meet and fall in love with Juliet, he dreads 'Some consequence, yet hanging in the stars' (line 107), which will cause 'untimely death' (line 111). Juliet fears this too at the end of her only night with Romeo. As she looks down at Romeo an image flashes through her mind of him 'dead in the bottom of a tomb' (Act 3 scene 5 line 56).

Work in a group of three

Discuss and make notes on the following:

1 Make a list of those things that Romeo and Juliet had little control over.

2 A number of events happen in the play which we could call bad luck. Write down these unfortunate events in the order in which they occur. Who was most to blame for each event?

3 Write down the names of five characters who were at least partly to blame for the deaths of Romeo and Juliet. Explain how each of those characters contributed to their deaths.

Authority

Verona is a hierarchical city. In other words, everyone has to obey someone else. There are strict rules about who you should look up to and respect. This means that people have to be obeyed because of who they are, not because they are right. At the top of the hierarchy is the Prince who is increasingly frustrated by the violent and disruptive feuding of his 'rebellious subjects' (Act 1 scene 1 line 80) – the Montagues and the Capulets. To assert his authority the Prince has awesome powers: he can banish people or even execute them.

At the head of the two warring families there is a patriarch, a male authority figure. At times Lord Capulet appears to be a kind and sensitive man, but he too asserts his authority when he is challenged. For example, at the party he humiliates his nephew, Tybalt, by ordering him to 'Be quiet' and leave Romeo alone (Act 1 scene 5 line 86). When Juliet refuses to marry Paris, Capulet flies into a fury and uses abuse and threats to force her to do his will.

The Prince, Capulet and Tybalt all use force to assert their authority. However, other characters in the play have authority without power. This is true of the Friar and – to some extent – the Nurse. Certainly the Friar commands respect on account of his wisdom. Even the Prince respects the Friar – so much so that when the Friar confesses his part in Romeo and Juliet's secret marriage the Prince forgives him with 'We still have known thee for a holy man.' (Act 5 scene 3 line 269)

Work with a partner

1 Draw a 'triangle of power' for Verona (see below).

2 Write characters' names at suitable points on the triangle.

3 Explain briefly why you have placed each character in your chosen position on the triangle. Would the characters occupy different positions on the triangles of authority, respect or wisdom?

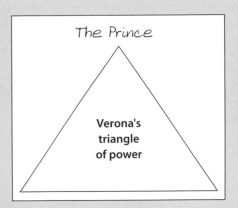

The Prince

Verona's triangle of power

Masculinity

Verona is a male-dominated society. The characters in positions of authority are all male and they expect women to obey them. This is seen most clearly in the relationship between Lord and Lady Capulet. Lord Capulet often gives his wife orders such as 'Prepare her, wife...' (Act 3 scene 4 line 32). Lady Capulet seems to have the status of a senior servant rather than an equal partner.

Not only are men in charge in Verona, but the notion of manliness is highly valued. At the start of the play, Romeo's conventional male aggression has been softened by his love for Rosaline. He now prefers quiet thought to fighting in the streets. Mercutio mocks him for his new dreaminess and condemns it as 'vain fantasy' (Act 1 scene 4 line 98). Romeo's dreamy sensitivity deepens when he meets Juliet. However, the traditional Verona notions of male honour are deeply ingrained in Romeo, and when Tybalt kills Mercutio, Romeo is disgusted with himself and blames Juliet for his 'softness': 'O sweet Juliet, | Thy beauty hath made me effeminate.' (Act 3 scene 1 lines 116–17)

Even Friar Lawrence accepts the conventional view that men should behave in particular ways: in Act 3 scene 3 when Romeo turns to the Friar in his distress, the Friar is appalled by Romeo's emotional state. He tells Romeo, 'Thy tears are womanish' (line 109) and accuses him of being an 'Unseemly woman in a seeming man' (line 111). The Nurse too believes that Romeo should fight his emotions: 'stand an [if] you be a man.' (Act 3 scene 3 line 88)

Work with a partner

1   Make two lists: things that you associate with being masculine; things that you associate with being feminine. Now add each of the following words to one list or the other:

brave   wise   good-looking
dominant   sensitive   loving

2   **Act 3 scene 5 lines 1–59**

    a Write down five words that sum up the way Romeo and Juliet speak to each other.

    b Is one of them the leader or do they view each other as equal partners? What makes you think this?

3   **Act 3 scene 5 lines 126–96**

    a Write down five words that sum up the way Lord and Lady Capulet speak to each other.

    b Compare the way Romeo and Juliet speak to each other with how Lord and Lady Capulet speak to each other. What are the main differences?

Conflict and reconciliation

Every aspect of life in Verona is plagued with conflict:

- The Prince struggles to control his 'rebellious subjects' (Act 1 scene 1 line 80).
- The Montagues and Capulets are locked into an 'ancient quarrel' (Act 1 scene 1 line 103) that results in regular killings.
- Mercutio feels let down by Romeo and they regularly engage in a 'match' of wits (Act 2 scene 4 line 71).
- Tybalt actively looks for fights and thrives on hatred:

> *What, drawn and talk of peace? I hate the word,*
> *As I hate hell, all Montagues, and thee.*
> (Act 1 scene 1 lines 68–9)

- Romeo and Juliet are torn between their sense of duty to their families and their desire for each other.

It is their accidental love for each other that makes Romeo and Juliet – and the audience – painfully aware of the eternal conflict that Verona is tragically caught up in. 'My only love sprung from my only hate' (Act 1 scene 5 line 137) is Juliet's anguished thought when she realises who Romeo is. There is a fatal contradiction between Juliet's love for Romeo and her family's ancient feud with Romeo's family.

This contradiction often rises to the surface of Juliet's language. For example, after Romeo kills Juliet's cousin, Juliet refers to Romeo in a series of images that include:

> Beautiful tyrant, fiend angelical,
> Dove-feathered raven, wolvish ravening lamb...
> (Act 3 scene 2 lines 75–6)

This kind of contradiction (How can a tyrant be 'beautiful'?) is very striking and is called an **oxymoron** (see Glossary p. 291).

Perhaps the cruellest conflict in the play is the one between the beauty and joy of Romeo and Juliet's love, and the terrible dark fate that awaits them. Romeo is bitterly aware of this contrast at the end of the play when he breaks into the tomb and finds Juliet still beautiful in the midst of death and decay:

> Death that hath sucked the honey of thy breath
> Hath had no power yet upon thy beauty.
> (Act 5 scene 3 lines 92–3)

It takes the tragic death of the young lovers to make the families finally realise the stupidity of their feud. Reconciliation finally happens when Lord Capulet says, 'O brother Montague, give me thy hand' (Act 5 scene 3 line 295) and Lord Montague pays the Capulets respect by promising to erect a commemorative statue to 'true and faithful Juliet' (Act 3 scene 5 line 301).

Conflict

Work with a partner

1   Look at the examples of conflict listed at the beginning of this section. Add at least three other examples of conflict in the play.

2   Choose two examples of conflict and make notes on these questions:

   a   Who is most to blame for each conflict?

   b   What impact does each conflict have on the action after that point?

Work on your own

3 What lessons do you think Shakespeare wants us to learn about conflict? Give reasons for your answer and refer to some evidence in the script.

The language of opposites

One way of expressing conflict is through **oxymorons**, the language of opposites. These images occur quite often in this play and help to give an edgy quality. They are used, for example, to express the contradictions and confusions that people sometimes feel when they fall in love.

Work with a partner

Look at Act 1 scene 1 lines 168–94. Make notes on the following:

1 Find three examples of **oxymoron** in Romeo's first speech.

2 Explain the contradiction in each one.

3 Choose one that you think shows how confused Romeo is and explain why you chose it.

4 In Romeo's second speech he uses other images to express his feelings. For example, he says that his griefs 'lie heavy' in his 'breast'. Find two other strong images from the speech. For each one, explain:

   a why you think it is strong

   b what you think it tells us about Romeo's state of mind at this point.

Writing about *Romeo and Juliet*

When you write about the play – even in a test – you should go through six stages:

1 **Read** the question and think about it.

2 **Develop** your ideas.

3 **Plan.**

4 **Write.**

5 **Edit** your writing.

6 **Check** that your writing is accurate.

Step 1: Read

The purpose of an assessment task is to give you the opportunity to discuss an aspect of the play in detail. In doing that you will show:

- your understanding of the play
- your appreciation of how it has been written and put together
- some idea of the play's relevance to its own time or ours.

You cannot write well about the play unless you understand the task fully. Look at this task:

> What do the last two scenes of Act 1 suggest about love and how it affects people's thoughts and behaviour?

The first thing to do is to identify the key words in the question. These are the words which show you exactly what the question is about. Here is the question again with the key words underlined:

> What do <u>the last two scenes of Act 1</u> suggest about <u>love</u> and how it affects people's <u>thoughts and behaviour</u>?

Now the point of the question becomes clear – it is about two main things in these two scenes:

- love
- the effects of love on people.

Step 2: Develop

Even in a test it is better to spend a few minutes planning your writing rather than rushing straight into it. Before you can make a plan, you need to develop your ideas. Start by writing down the question's key words on a clean page.

Then jot down thoughts that might be relevant to those key words and the given scenes.

Now use lines to mark possible links between your thoughts, turning them into a sort of web of ideas.

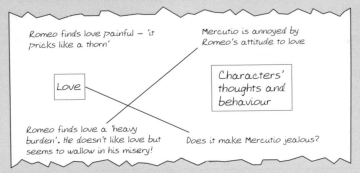

Add pieces of evidence (for example, short quotations) that you might be able to use in your writing to support your ideas, but also be prepared to cross out thoughts that don't seem to fit in very well.

Step 3: Plan

Now you need to shape your ideas into a plan. This provides the structure, or order, of your writing.

1 You need an introduction that explains:

a what the task means for you

b why this topic is an important one.

Think about what love is and what it does in this play. However, don't answer the question yet; just get your reader interested! Here is an example of a lively and direct opening:

> In these two scenes we are given different views of love and the effect it has on characters. Whether he is sad or happy, Romeo always seems to be under the control of love. He seems to be helpless under its influence.

2 At the end of the answer you need a concluding paragraph. This sums up your most important points and answers the question directly.

3 Now for the tricky part: you need a series of paragraphs that bridge the gap between the introduction and the conclusion. Look back at the question and at the ideas you have come up with in your diagram. This will help you with the main points you need to cover before answering the question in your conclusion.

What to do	Focus on	Paragraph topic
It makes sense to begin with the scene that comes first in the play. So you need a paragraph for each of the main characters in that scene – Romeo and Mercutio – and how each responds to love.	Act 1 scene 4	1. Romeo
		2. Mercutio
Now you can move to the other scene and write about Romeo and Juliet	Act 1 scene 5	3. Romeo
		4. Juliet
Finally you can look at similarities and differences between how these characters are affected by love.	Both scenes together	5. Similarities
		6. Differences

Step 4: Draft

Whatever the writing task, you need to explore most of these things:

- the play's ideas and meaning
- its structure
- its characters
- audience (or reader) reaction
- stagecraft: how the play is performed
- the language of the play.

Point, Evidence, and Explanation

It is easy to become vague when you are writing. Planning will help you to stick to the point and to organise your ideas so that you develop and explain them rather than keep repeating them.

PEE – point, evidence, and explanation – is a useful formula for expressing your ideas clearly. Here is an example:

> When Romeo meets Juliet he immediately presents his love as something holy [POINT]: he uses the religious words 'profane', 'shrine', 'sin', etc [EVIDENCE] This might mean that Romeo wants to show Juliet deep respect. Comparing his feelings with religious worship would do that. Of course, his extended religious metaphor could just be a very clever chat-up line to impress Juliet! [EXPLANATION].

To explore ideas and evidence try to use words such as *could, might, perhaps*. These help you explore more than one possibility – as in the example above.

Step 5: Edit

When you have finished your first draft you should read through your work carefully to make sure it actually says what you mean. As you read it through, try to imagine that you are the person who will mark it. What would they think of what you have written? Ask yourself:

- Have I used Point, Evidence, Explanation?
- Do all my sentences make sense?

- Are the sentences vague, or are they clear and to the point?
- Have I missed anything out?
- Is everything relevant to the task?
- Make any changes needed.

Step 6: Check

When you are satisfied with your answer, make a final check for:

- grammar
- punctuation
- spelling.

Writing tasks and questions

The following varied writing tasks are all designed to allow you to show:

- your understanding of the play
- your appreciation of how it has been written and put together
- some idea of the play's relevance to its own time or ours.

Look carefully at each task and work out what each one is asking for. Underline the key words for a start.

1 A key theme in *Romeo and Juliet* is the relationship between love and marriage. What do Act 1 scene 3 and Act 3 scene 5 suggest about this topic?

2 In Act 1 we learn a lot about the relationship between Romeo and Benvolio. If you were directing the play, what detailed advice would you give to the actors playing these two roles about how to tackle Act 1 scene 1 and Act 1 scene 2?

3 What impressions do we gain of Juliet from what she says and does in Act 2 scene 2 and Act 4 scene 3?

4 How does Romeo's language show his different feelings in Act 1 scene 5 lines 41–5 and Act 5 scene 3 lines 58–120?

5   Imagine that at the end of Act 3 scene 1 the Prince holds an inquest into the deaths of Mercutio and Tybalt. Write the newspaper report of the inquest. Refer in detail to:

   a   what witnesses say about the fight

   b   their attitudes to what happened

   c   what might have been said and done earlier in the play that might be relevant.

6   Imagine you are a magazine writer who specialises in giving advice on family and relationships. You are asked to write an article about Romeo and Juliet to consider the lessons we should learn from their tragic experience. Write the article.

7   Choose any two of the older characters in the play and explain how their behaviour or attitudes contributed to the tragic deaths of Romeo and Juliet.

8   Choose any two of the following characters. Compare and contrast their attitudes towards love.

   a   Romeo

   b   Mercutio

   c   Capulet

   d   Nurse

   e   Friar Lawrence

9   Some people criticise the second half of the play because there are so many coincidences. Others say that this is the whole point: Shakespeare wanted to show how fate worked in the lives of Romeo and Juliet, and fate works through coincidence. Who do you think is right, and why?

Glossary

In these explanations, words that are in **bold** type are explained separately in this Glossary.

alliteration   a figure of speech in which words close to each other in a piece of writing begin with the same consonant sound: '...you fiery-footed steeds...' (Act 3 scene 2 line 1) The repeated 'f' and 't' sounds help to draw attention to these words.

apostrophe   a figure of speech in which a character speaks directly to a person who is not present or to a **personification**. For example, when Juliet says, 'O fortune, fortune, all men call thee fickle' (Act 3 scene 5 line 60), she is talking to the personification of fortune.

aside   a speech made by one of the characters for the ears of the audience alone, or purely for the benefit of another character on stage. For example in Act 3 scene 5, when Juliet's mother calls Romeo a villain, Juliet says 'Villain and he be many miles asunder...' (line 81) This is said to the audience and her mother is not supposed to be able to hear it. See also **soliloquy**.

blank verse   Shakespeare wrote his plays using a mixture of prose and verse. The lines of verse sometimes **rhymed** but more often did not rhyme. Verse that does not rhyme is called blank verse.

caesura   a pause or interruption in the middle of a line of verse (from the Latin word meaning 'to cut'). For example, in Act 3 scene 5 Juliet has the lines: 'If thou art fickle, what dost thou with him | That is renowned for faith? Be fickle, fortune;' (lines 61–2) In the first line the caesura comes after 'fickle', and in the second after 'faith'.

contraction	shortening a word or words by missing out some of the letters. The missing letters are shown by an apostrophe. Modern examples are *she's* (for *she is*) and *shan't* (for *shall not*). In Shakespeare's time other contractions were also used, such as *'tis* (for *it is*) and *show'st* (for *showest*).
dramatic irony	a situation in a play when the audience (and possibly some of the characters) knows something one or more of the characters do not. In a pantomime for example, young children will often shout to tell the hero that a dreadful monster is creeping up behind him, unseen. For example in Act 2 scene 2, Juliet voices her love for Romeo not realising that he is listening. The audience knows that he is, so they know the effect of her words on him, even though she doesn't.
end-on staging	a form of staging in which the audience sit in rows all facing the same way with the stage at one end.
enjambement	sometimes in blank verse there is a natural pause at the end of a line. At other times there is no break and the sentence just runs over onto the next line: 'If thou art fickle, what dost thou with him I That is renowned for faith?' (Act 3 scene 5 lines 61–2) This running-on is called enjambement (from the French word for 'span').
exeunt	a Latin word meaning 'They go away', used for the departure of characters from a scene.
exit	a Latin word meaning 'He (or she) goes away', used for the departure of a character from a scene.
extended image	most **images** are fairly short, taking up no more than a line or two. Sometimes a writer builds up

an image so that it runs on for several lines. This is called an extended image. For example in Act 1 scene 5 Romeo and Juliet develop the idea that their love-at-first-sight is holy: Juliet is a 'holy shrine' (line 93); Romeo's lips are 'pilgrims' (line 94); their first kiss is a 'prayer' (line 101).

figurative language   language used that is not literally true, usually for some kind of special effect. **Metaphors** and **similes** are examples of figurative language.

hyperbole   deliberate exaggeration, for dramatic effect. For example, in Act 2 scene 2, Romeo says, 'My bounty is as boundless as the sea, | My love as deep' (lines 133–4)

iambic pentameter   a line of **verse** which contains ten syllables, with a repeated pattern of weak and strong beats:
In **fair** Ver**o**na **where** we **lay** our **scene**
(ti **tum** ti **tum** ti **tum** ti **tum** ti **tum**)
(Prologue, line 2)
See also **metre**, **rhythm**.

imagery   **figurative language** in which the writer communicates an idea by creating a picture in the mind of the reader or listener. Types of figurative language include **metaphors** and **similes**.

irony   when someone says one thing and means another. Sometimes it is used to tease or satirise someone or it can express great bitterness. For example in Act 1 scene 5 Lord Capulet mocks Tybalt for daring to try take control of who should be allowed to be at the party: 'you'll be the man?' he asks Tybalt sarcastically (line 80).
See also **dramatic irony**.

metaphor   a figure of speech in which one person, or thing, or idea is described as if it were another. For example, Mercutio calls Tybalt 'King of Cats' (Act 3 scene 1 line 78). He does not mean this literally; what he really means is that Tybalt is proud, always preening himself, and survives the many fights he gets into.

metre
the regular pattern of weak and strong beats in a line of verse. The most common metre in Shakespeare's plays is iambic. Each section consists of two syllables. The first is weak and the second is strong. See **iambic pentameter.**

oxymoron
figurative language in which the writer combines two ideas which are opposites. This frequently has a startling or unusual effect: For example in Act 1 scene 5 Romeo describes touching Juliet as a 'gentle sin' (line 93). 'Gentle' and 'sin' conflict in a thought-provoking way.

personification
referring to a thing or an idea as if it were a person. For example, when Juliet says, 'O fortune, fortune, all men call thee fickle' (Act 3 scene 5 line 60), she is talking to an abstract idea (fortune, or chance) as if it were a person.

play on words
see **pun.**

prose
the form of language that is used for normal written communication. It is contrasted with **verse**.

proverb
a common saying that is used by many people. Proverbs usually express something that is useful knowledge, or that people think is useful. For example, 'Many hands make light work'. Some famous quotations from *Romeo and Juliet* have become proverbs in their own right, for example:

'a rose | By any other word would smell as sweet'. (Act 2 scene 2 line 43–4).

pun a figure of speech in which the writer uses a word that has more than one meaning. Both meanings of the word are used to make a joke. There is a lot of punning in *Romeo and Juliet*, especially when Mercutio is around, for example Act 2 scene 4 lines 51–88.

rhetorical question a question used for effect, usually in argument or debate, or sometimes in a soliloquy. An answer is not expected; it would break the flow of the speech if it were offered. For example, Juliet says, 'Tybalt's dead, that would have slain my husband. | All this is comfort, wherefore weep I then?' (Act 3 scene 2 lines 106–7)

rhyme when two lines of verse end with the same sound, they are said to rhyme. Shakespeare often makes use of rhyme, both in the middle of scenes and to round them off. For example, Act 1 scene 2 ends with Romeo saying: 'I'll go along, no such sight to be shown, | But to rejoice in splendour of mine own.' (lines 101–2)

rhythm the pattern of weak and strong syllables in a piece of writing. Shakespeare writes in **iambic pentameters**, but varies the way he uses them by breaking the rules. So his lines are mainly regular but with a lot of small variations. This combination makes up the rhythm of the verse. For example in Act 3 scene 5 (lines 176–9) Capulet expresses his anger like this:
God's bread, it makes me mad.
Day, night, hour, tide, time, work, play,
Alone, in company, still my care hath been
To have her matched

The broken, jerky rhythm of the speech expresses the way his anger is boiling up.

satire
making fun of something that you dislike or wish to criticise, by sending it up in some way.

simile
a comparison between two things which the writer makes clear by using words such as 'like' or 'as'. For example, when Romeo first sees Juliet he says she is 'like a rich jewel' (Act 1 Scene 5 line 45).

soliloquy
when a character is alone on stage, or separated from the other characters in some way and speaks either apparently to himself or herself, or directly to the audience. For example at the end of Act 4 scene 3, Juliet is left alone in her bedroom and prepares to take the potion Friar Lawrence has given her. She has a long soliloquy in which she expresses her doubts about what she has to do (lines 14–58).

theatre-in-the-round
a form of theatre in which the audience sit on all sides of the acting area.

thrust stage
a form of theatre in which the stage projects out into the audience, who thus sit on three sides of it. Shakespeare's Globe theatre was like this, and so is the modern one in London, and the new Royal Shakespeare Theatre in Stratford-upon-Avon.

verse
writing that uses regular patterns, such as **metre** and **rhyme**.